THIS WAS AIR TRAVEL

THIS WAS AIR TRAVEL

by

Henry R. Palmer, Jr.

BONANZA BOOKS · NEW YORK

START OF AN AERIAL JAUNT. Captain Thomas Baldwin and the Hudson balloon, Central Park, San Francisco, 1895.

This book is dedicated to the memory of those remarkable men who made the airplane a reality—Orville and Wilbur Wright.

FOREWORD

OVER the edge of a basket suspended from an ornately decorated bag filled with hot air, two men looked down on a gaping throng and embraced themselves. The year was 1783. The place was the Chateau de la Muette, Paris. The men were Pilatre de Rozier and the Marquis d'Arlandes—the first humans to rise off the earth.

Ever since that epochal balloon ascension, man's driving urge to conquer the pull of gravity has continued, and with each triumph the challenge becomes greater, but always with the same goal—to carry more people aloft, higher, faster, farther. This book portrays some of the intriguing methods and wonderful devices used to meet these challenges.

This is not a history of aviation nor a record of all the flying machines that have clattered and roared down through the years. But rather it is a simple presentation of a nostalgic panorama of early balloons and dirigibles and airplanes whose performances have been historically important.

The earliest planes of the pre-World War I period were flimsy affairs. Designers continually confronted with the problem of how to save weight, cut here and skimped there, using only the lightest woods and cloths. Seldom did planes of the day withstand more than a few weeks of hard abuse, and rare was the one that lasted longer. Because of this, scarcely a handful of ancient planes exist today. Those that remain, historically important in their pioneering achievements, sit out their lives in museums. Of the thousands originally built, the sole link between the past and the present is the photograph whose importance increases as these delicate relics crumble away one by one.

As the knowledge of airplane design and construction advanced, stronger and more durable materials appeared, and by the late Nineteen Twenties metal had begun to replace fabric.

All-metal planes, properly cared for, might be expected to last indefinitely, but they could not survive the rapid advancements in design which rendered them obsolete long before their time. It seems unjust that so many superb flying machines should be forced into early retirement and the wrecker's yard but this is the price of progress. The wanton destruction of healthy, safe and sound aircraft has been going on for years and will continue as long as travelers demand, and engineers supply, the fastest and the finest in transportation.

A few of the early all-metal planes have survived extinction in spite of the fearful competition—a handful of Ford *Tri-Motors,* a few thousand *DC-3s,* some Lockheed *Lodestars* and *Electras.* There are others. But for every pre-1940 aircraft flying today, thousands have disappeared. And soon they will all disappear, for already we have entered the age of supersonic jet aircraft and guided missiles and face an era of inter-planetary travel.

Now is the time to take stock of what man has so far created.

Henry R. Palmer, Jr.

CONTENTS

MAN STRUGGLES TO FLY

DOWN through the ages men marveled at the mysterious force that glued them to the earth, and they yearned for the ability to rise above it and fly like the birds.

To the ancient traveler, with no means of transportation other than his two feet or a plodding horse or camel to cover the endless roadless expanses, or a clumsy boat that went only where the wind or oars took it, the desire to soar through the air must have become an obsession.

What he failed to accomplish in reality he imagined, creating ethereal characters that dominated the religions, the thinking, the beliefs of men for countless centuries.

Hundreds of years before Christ, the Chinese had conjured up illusions of a flying chariot drawn through the heavens by a fair wind. The Assyrians had created flying bulls. The Persians visioned their king transporting himself through the sky in an eagle-propelled throne.

The Romans invented Mercury, the winged messenger of the gods. The Greeks believed Apollo carried the sun across the heavens in his flying chariot, that Icarus flew on wings of feathers in 1100 BC. Other legends and fables involved seven league boots, flying carpets, fairy godmothers, angels, halloween witches, Santa Claus—all imagination but expressive of man's intense yearning to rise above the earth in continuous flight.

But mortal beings seemed destined to remain forever earth-bound until one evening in 1782 a man in France made a momentous discovery. Sitting before his open fire he watched the rising smoke carry bits of paper and straw and ash up his chimney. Suddenly amazed at the great power exerted by the air, he determined to harness it in some manner, wondering if by chance this might be the medium to take man aloft.

Fashioning a paper bag he held it over the fire, allowing it to fill with the warm air. Quickly taking it out of the fireplace he released it, and to his utter astonishment watched it climb slowly to the ceiling.

Joseph Montgolfier had created the first balloon, an event destined to change the entire course of world affairs.

By June of the following year, Joseph and his brother Etienne had built and tested a balloon of nearly 24,000 cubic feet capacity, 38 feet in diameter. They made it of paper-lined linen and filled it with hot air from a fire built under a platform on which it rested. Cast off when filled, it rose nearly 6000 feet, drifted gently back to earth and landed in a field a mile away where terrified peasants tore it apart with pitchforks.

And finally, man himself was carried aloft for the first time. In a magnificently decorated balloon holding 100,000 cubic feet of hot air, 85 feet long and 48 feet in diameter, two men ascended like gods themselves from the launching platform in the gardens of the Chateau de la Muette in Paris before a half million awed spectators. Standing in a gallery that encircled the throat of the massive bag, they doffed their hats politely to the crowd as they climbed triumphantly skyward. A small brazier stretched across the gaping mouth of the balloon provided additional hot air to extend its cruising radius. The occupants fed the fire with bits of wool and shavings when they wished to climb, allowing it to die down when they chose to lose altitude.

For five miles a gentle breeze carried them across Paris, and 27 minutes after blast off they landed gracefully in a field near the city, unhurt and tumultuously acclaimed. Man had finally flown.

The following year the Montgolfiers built a huge balloon that carried seven people aloft at once. By 1785 the English Channel had been crossed, the first woman passenger had been carried, the first fatalities had occurred. By 1794 a balloon had gone to war doing artillery spotting for Napoleon. Now a French strategist envisioned sending entire armies to invade England in balloons carrying 3000 men apiece, but this was fanciful dreaming; during the siege of Paris, 66 balloons of 70,000 cubic foot capacity apiece flew 102 passengers, a quantity of homing pigeons and ten tons of mail out of the beleaguered city.

By 1804 the altitude record stood at 22,892 feet. Twenty years later three men flew non-stop for 480 miles—a stupendous event that did much to solidify the public's wavering opinion of aerostation in general. And in 1863, fifteen people took off together in a huge balloon known simply and effectively as the "Giant."

In place of the usual wicker basket, "Giant" carried a car 7 feet high, 13 feet wide and 25 feet long, probably the first aerial cabin. Designed for extensive cruising, it contained seats for the passengers, a captain's room, a stateroom with three berths, a larder, lavatory and photographic room. There were windows in its side and an observation deck on top. And because a possibility existed that this great vehicle might force land in some remote area, pro-visions were made on the car to fit it with wheels and axles so it might be dragged to the nearest habitation without disturbing its passengers.

"Giant" made a number of successful flights, and on one occasion demonstrated its great lifting ability by carrying 30 passengers at once.

Probably the greatest balloon of all however, was an 880,000 cubic foot monster used at the French International exposition in 1878. Carrying 50 people at a time, it was restrained from climbing higher than 1600 feet by strong ropes and a powerful steam winch, thereby offering a comparatively safe and comfortable method for the curious to fly, while still keeping one foot on the ground. During the four months of the Exposition, it carried more than 35,000 people aloft.

DRUM AND RETAINING ROPES of steam-driven winch used to control "flight" of Giffard's captive balloon in Paris.

FIFTY FRENCHMEN COULDN'T BE WRONG (opposite). Henri Giffard's great captive balloon at the 1878 Paris Exposition. Note ramp leading to 50-passenger car and six massive retaining lines that gave passengers hold on earth.

BALLOONING IN ENGLAND

SHORTLY after the turn of the century, ballooning became a major sport among the wealthy in Europe and England. Racing and cross country flights (both day and night) were immensely popular among the members of this exclusive fraternity and the weekend meets at Hurlingham and Ranelagh placed high up on the social calendar.

The average pleasure balloon of the day contained 80,000 cubic feet of gas, carried four people and cost in the neighborhood of $1200.00. Passengers stood in the wicker basket throughout the flight ascending by releasing sand from the bags suspended around the basket's sides, and descending by valving off gas. An anchor and a long length of stout rope served to pull the car safely to earth at journey's end. Standard equipment usually consisted of a sensitive barometer to tell height above sea level, a compass and a statoscope, an instrument that registered small variations of atmospheric pressure. Food and water, warm clothes and possibly a blanket or two completed the airship's gear.

Because balloons move only with the wind, occupants rode undisturbed by any air flow, floating through the air so silently that noises below could be heard distinctly at many hundreds of feet of altitude.

Balloons of this type were generally inflated with household illuminating gas, which, although no safer than hydrogen and lacking much of the latter's lift, could be readily obtained at relatively low cost.

ADS OF THE DAY. Pioneer Baldwin advertises to an awakening public—and who remembers the Buchet motor? For that matter, who would want a used balloon? Leo Stevens was in a growing business and a dollar went a long way.

MIXED FOURSOME SOARS UPWARD. Two men and female companions set off on cross country race over a midsummer countryside in England, 1912.

THREE STOUT-HEARTED WOMEN and two men prepare to take off in balloon contest—Hurlingham, England, July 13, 1912. Note anchor line snuggled up alongside, sand bags, statoscope and retaining lines.

FLY-BY, 1913 VERSION. Britain's airship *Gamma* creeps past admiring crowd at Laffan's Plain, England, on King's birthday.

THE POWERED GAS BAGS

BALLOONS possessed one great fault, which limited their usefulness to little more than sport: they could not be steered. Aeronauts tried doggedly to solve this problem, attempting many a freakish and outlandish idea all without success. Yet the efforts persisted and in 1852 a controllable airship appeared. A fish-shaped bag 143 feet long and about as rigid as a piece of rope, it was propelled by a 3 HP steam engine, and steered by a crude sail. In a flat calm, engine wide open, its top speed approached 7 miles per hour. It was not a great success but a step in the right direction.

Others followed: one powered by eight men turning a propeller with a hand crank; another by a single occupant spinning the prop with foot pedals. By 1880 a gasoline engine had been used with some success, and four years later, successful flights were made in an airship that looked like a badly broken cigar, driven through the air at a smart 7 mile per hour clip by a 9 HP electric motor. But the real honors went to Alberto Santos-Dumont who produced a whole fleet of controllable airships.

This charming little Brazilian, who wore bizarre-looking hats and tall stiff collars, cheerfully risked his life time after time in his fantastic floppy gas bags, to the intense joy of doting Parisians. By 1901 he had won a 25000 franc prize by flying Number 6 from St. Cloud around the Eiffel tower and back—nine miles in 29½ minutes. Santos-Dumont created enormous interest in aeronautics and became a national hero of France. In all, he constructed 13 lighter-than-air machines in various sizes and shapes.

And then came Germany's Count Ferdinand Zeppelin, whose name was to become synonymous with all dirigibles. In the summer of 1900 the first of the long line of these immense airships, 425 feet long, lifted from the waters of Lake Constance, climbed to 1300 feet and flew at a sedate eight miles per hour for 20 minutes, while the dumfounded multitudes below gasped and exclaimed over the wonder they were beholding.

For it was indeed a great wonder, this "rigid" airship—the first ever built. Its shape was formed by an aluminum trusswork completely covered inside and out with specially-treated linen and silk. Seventeen individual cells within held the nearly 350,000 cubic feet of hydrogen which lifted the 10 ton craft.

Two aluminum cars, one at each end of the ship, housed a 16 HP Daimler benzine engine. Each turned twin 4-bladed propellers. A rudder controlled lateral movement, while a sliding weight directed it vertically.

As is so often the case with new inventions, *LZ-1* was not entirely successful, although subsequent ones showed marked improvement. More power in the *LZ-2* gave it additional speed. *LZ-3* made 38 miles per hour with complete maneuverability. *LZ-4* triumphed. With a capacity of better than 500,000 cubic feet of hydrogen, and powered by two engines developing a total of 220 HP, it succeeded in carrying 12 people on one 12 hour flight in 1908. A month later it completed one of 20 hours. By 1909, *LZ-5* flew for 38 hours non stop, and so it went. The future for lighter-than-air could not have looked brighter. That year Count Zeppelin and young Dr. Hugo Eckener created Deutsche Luftschiffahrts-Aktien-Gesellschaft, the first scheduled airline the world had known. With airports located in Friedrichshafen, Frankfurt, Hamburg, Leipzig, Potsdam and Dresden, DELAG commenced regular passenger service in 1910 using the great dirigible *Deutschland 1,* which could accommodate 20 people in its rosewood-lined aluminum cabin.

Deutschland 1's life as a passenger carrier was a short one, however, for a week later she crashed head on into the Teutoburg Forest. Fortunately for the new company, no one was injured, and service soon resumed with the *Schwaben,* later followed by the *Hansa, Viktoria-Louise* and *Sachsen.*

For five years these big ships shuttled around Germany, carrying over 37,000 passengers in 3200 hours of scheduled flying time, a record unmarred by a single injury to anyone.

But with the advent of war, DELAG's future suddenly blackened and died. All operations ceased for the duration. Fourteen years would lapse before a war-devastated Germany could resume a full scale lighter-than-air passenger service.

AS OTHERS SEE US. Two aeronauts photograph themselves by remote control in balloon over Paris in 1914.

PRE-WAR TRANSPORT. *Schwaben,* German dirigible — Zeppelin's second DELAG airship, carried over 2,000 passengers in four months of scheduled flying in 1911. *Schwaben* was 490 feet long, 46 feet wide, carried 5 ton payload at 43 miles per hour. Built expressly for passenger work, luxurious main cabin rivaled Pullman car comfort.

LIGHTER-THAN-AIR TRANSPORTATION. Passengers, including several women, board DELAG's dirigible *Deutschland 1,* first of Zeppelins to enter commercial service in Germany—1910.

AERIAL TROLLEY CAR. Passenger cabin on *Deutschland 1* seating 20 with unobstructed view for all.

END OF A FLIGHT. Roy Knabenshue eases his airship over fence in New York's Central Park after flight during summer, 1905. "So great was the curiosity of the New Yorkers to view the flights," reported Scientific American Sept. 2, 1905 "that almost all business and street traffic was at a standstill and throngs followed the course of the great dirigible balloon hovering over the city." *Toledo II* was 69 feet long, contained 7,000 cubic feet of hydrogen, was propelled by 10 HP air-cooled gasoline engine which turned 10 foot diameter propeller at about 150 RPM.

BIRD'S EYE VIEW OF CHICAGO. Four passengers appear relaxed and unafraid of their high perch over Lake Michigan.

DEUTSCHLAND OBER ALLES—1912. *Viktoria Luise,* operated by DELAG in Germany, carried hundreds of passengers on over 200 trips ranging from 10 to 20 hours each. Keynotes of success of these aerial leviathans stemmed from great steadiness and airworthiness.

AMERICAN STYLE AIRSHIP OVER CHICAGO—1914. U.S. was rank amateur compared to Germany in lighter-than-air ship design. This carrot-shaped blimp, created by American aeronaut Roy Knabenshue made history however in 1913 and 1914 doing aerial sightseeing through Middle West.

THE WRIGHTS

UPON completion of Orville Wright's first flight at Kitty Hawk, N. C. on the morning of December 17, 1903, the age of the powered flying machine had come at last.

For four years the Wrights had been working on the problems of flight, studying, experimenting with materials, even testing wing shapes in a wind tunnel created by them for the purpose. They built man-carrying gliders in their shop at Dayton, Ohio, and flew them at Kitty Hawk, chosen because it met their requirements of a place where steady winds blew over a large expanse unbroken by trees and hills which might have tended to create disturbances in the air and make gliding difficult.

The 1902 glider made hundreds of flights that summer, and proved to be capable of remarkably flat glides—as little as five degrees below horizontal. The door was open to them, and they immediately began the design and construction of the 1903 ma-chine, destined to become the most famous aeroplane in the world.

This was a biplane, a type selected because its truss-like construction of bracing wires and struts offered the greatest amount of strength for the least span of lifting surface. It was powered by a Wright-built 4 cylinder 12 HP engine connected by roller chains to two huge pusher propellers.

Considering the fact that neither Orville nor Wilbur had previously flown it is remarkable that they were able to keep their new machine in the air as long as they did. It was a cold winter morning with the wind blowing between 25 and 30 miles per hour, hardly ideal conditions for an experiment of this magnitude, and yet they accomplished four flights ranging from 12 seconds for the first, to 59 for the last. A total of one minute and 36 seconds was ac-cumulated on the machine whereupon it was retired for life.

WORLD'S MOST FAMOUS PLANE. 1903 Wright pusher—first to take off, fly and land under complete control of pilot. Now in Smithsonian Museum, frail machine collected total flying time of one minute, thirty-six seconds.

WRIGHTS FLY HIGH (above) far and long at Dayton, Ohio, 1905 and still not another soul in the world had become airborne in anything heavier than air.

FIRST SUCCESSFUL AIRPLANE ENGINE 4-cyl. water-cooled Wright used in the Dec. 17, 1903 flights. Weighing 179 pounds, it developed 15 HP at 1,200 RPM, was started on ground with dry battery whereupon magneto provided ignition. Speed on ground was regulated by retarding spark, no way to control it in flight.

24

A TRIP WITH WILBUR WRIGHT

By Major Baden-Powell, Ed. "Aeronautics"

(Reprinted from "Aeronautics," Dec. 1908)

"MANY accounts have recently been published describing the aeroplane machine with which Mr. Wilbur Wright has been making such very successful flights during the last few weeks.

"It is, however, quite a different matter reading such descriptions to actually seeing the apparatus and watching it fly in the air. It is again a still further revelation to get into the air car and experience an actual flight. Four Englishmen have been lucky enough to undergo the latter experience during last month. These are Mr. Griffith Brewer, the Hon. C. S. Rolls, Mr. Frank Butler and myself.

"The first feeling that one experiences on seeing the machine in operation are surprise and almost disappointment at the absolute regularity with which everything seems to work. No exciting incidents, no laughable mistakes, no delays mar the usual routine.

"It may be of interest to describe in detail the various operations, and incidentally to show that this machine, while acting so satisfactorily, so perfectly, yet is very crude and even clumsy as regards many of its fittings and appendages.

"The machine is trailed off to the starting place, perhaps a couple of hundred yards from the shed, and is drawn over the starting rail. The latter consists of a series of upright wooden planks, with an iron band along the top fixed end to end. It is about 100 feet long, and is laid in the direction of the wind and pegged to the ground.

"Now the little trolley is placed on the track and carefully adjusted under the center of the lower aeroplane. This trolley consists of a piece of wood about two feet long with a roller attached at each end. Across the center of this runs a stout beam, like a railway sleeper on the ends of which the whole machine rests. A small roller on the frame of the machine also rests on the rail supporting the weight of the fore planes. Why all these wheels should not be permanently attached to the machine I do not know. They could be very lightly made.

"Then the big wheels have to be unlashed and removed. The whole machine is then resting only on the little rollers of the trolley, so, to keep it upright, the end of the lower aeroplane has to be supported on a trestle placed temporarily underneath it.

"A few yards behind the near end of the starting rail is the 'pylon,' consisting of four upright beams braced together, 25 feet high, with a large pulley slung at the top.

"A heavy weight, consisting of about six large discs of iron, weighing 220 pounds each, is hooked on and drawn up to the top by a long rope passing round the pulley, and led from the bottom of the tower to the track. This operation is done either by a number of men hauling on the rope, or the latter is attached to a motor car, which moves off and draws up the weights.

"The end of the rope . . . is attached to a hook on the aeroplane. The latter is temporarily anchored to the track by a loop of wire held by a small lever catch.

"The engines are now started by two men turning the propellers together. Mr. Wright generally lets the motor run for some minutes while he carefully watches it and examines all parts to see that everything is correct.

"Then comes the exciting moment for the passenger to take his seat. Having clambered in among various rods and wires one struggles into the little seat arranged on the front edge of the lower plane, and places one's feet on a small bar in front. A string is found crossing just in front of one's chest, and Mr. Wright gives directions that this must not be touched. It is a simple contrivance for cutting off the ignition and stopping the engine. In event of any accident, the body will probably be thrown forward, and pressing against the string, immediately stops the engine. Once Mr. Wright put up his hand to adjust his cap while in mid-air, and accidentally touched the string, and the machine landed unexpectedly (though of course quite smoothly).

"All being ready, coats are buttoned, and caps pulled down to prevent being blown off. In one trip the passenger's cap was blown off and caught in one of the wire stays behind. Although the chains transmitting the power to the propellers are enclosed in tubes for most of their length, it seems possible that a cap might fall foul of them and be drawn into the gearing, which might have an awkward effect.

"Then the driver bends down and releases the catch which holds the anchoring wire. The machine is off! It bounds forward and travels rapidly along the rail. The fore planes are meanwhile pressed down to prevent the machine lifting prematurely, but when about half the length of the rail has been traversed, the lever is pulled back, the planes come into operation, and the whole machine rises, almost imperceptibly off the track. But in the case of my first trip, all did not go well. The object of the starting device is to get up a sufficient speed to enable the aeroplane to rise in the air. If the speed is not quite sufficient the machine soon falls to the ground. Now, just as we started, a light puff of wind struck the apparatus, not from the front, which would have been advantageous, but from the side. The result was that we did not get sufficient impetus, and, after a jump through the air, landed on the runners.

"This seemed disappointing, but it was an experience. It gave one an idea of the sensations of the start, and proved how easy and soft was the landing, even when unexpected.

"The machine having landed, although within quite a short distance of the starting point, the wheels had to be fetched, placed in position, and lashed on, and the machine is wheeled back for a fresh start to be made.

"Then, the same processes having been gone through, a better start was made. From experience with bicycles and low powered motors we can all realize how greatly a slight upward gradient detracts from the speed and calls for extra power, but one is apt to forget that the same applies to the flyer. The ascent must be very gradual. When the machine leaves the

track it glides so close to the ground that one often doubts if it is really started in the air, but then it gradually mounts and steadily proceeds on its journey.

"So steady and regular is the motion that it appears exactly as if it were progressing along on an invisible elevated track. Only just now and again, as a swirl of wind catches it, does it make a slight undulation like a boat rising to a big wave. Mr. Wright, with both hands grasping the levers, watches every move, but his movements are so slight as to be almost imperceptible. Having soon reached the end of the ground, the machine is guided round in a large semicircle, gracefully leaning over as it turns, just as a large soaring bird would do.

"Back she comes the whole length of the ground, sometimes keeping exactly on a level with the tree tops, sometimes she descends and moves along five or six feet above the ground. All the time the engines are buzzing loudly and the propellers humming so that after a trip one is almost deaf.

"Again the machine swoops round and returns past the group of onlookers at the starting point. On it goes, as steadily as ever, always the same under perfect control.

"Then at last the run is completed. The machine is brought down close to the ground. It skims along only a foot or two above the sandy plain. Then the ignition is cut off, the propellers stop, and the machine lands on its skids, shooting for some distance along the ground."

BIPLANE BUILT FOR TWO. This 1908 Wright accommodated pilot and passenger in tiny seat attached to leading edge of lower wing. Planes did not have seat belts in these days and passenger clung to struts as best he could. Pilot, occupied with plane's controls, relied on luck, smooth air and grace of God to keep him on his perch.

GLENN MARTIN FLIES HIS PUSHER. He used this 1912 model considerably for exhibition flying which included racing automobiles.

THIS IS COMFORT? Youthful Joe E. Brown, well-known American comedian, nervously clutches wing braces of early Martin biplane as he perches behind Glenn L. Martin before taking off on adventurous ride. Even most enthusiastic birdmen dared not dream of regular on-the-minute schedules for flights across borders and oceans but this type of flying did have color and adventure.

WINGS SPROUT ABROAD

AFTER the turn of the century, a handful of men in Europe struggled with the weighty problems of flight. Little was known of the Wright brothers and their achievements for they were secretive men, and until they could be sure of their patent rights, were reluctant to let the world know of their progress. Rumors of their accomplishments emanating from the United States were taken with a grain of salt.

With no help from this aeronautical progress, these European pioneers—Voisin, Santos-Dumont, the Farmans, Bleriot and others—carried on their own experiments. Alberto Santos-Dumont, who had been astounding France with his fantastic dirigibles, became the first to fly a powered aeroplane. His machine,

known simply as *Bis 14,* was a clumsy, box-kite contraption, composed mainly of bamboo and silk, possessing the peculiar distinction of flying tail first.

By 1906 the secret of flight was out, and others soon followed. Records began to fall with amazing rapidity: the first turn, the first woman to fly, figure eights, carrying the first passenger. In June 1909 the altitude record stood at 450 feet and the fastest speed was 58 miles per hour. At the August 10 Rheims meet, no less than nine machines were seen in the air at once. In America, Wilbur Wright circled the Statue of Liberty while Glenn Curtiss flew around Governor's Island. And so it went.

By 1911 the aeroplane had come into its own and

TIME FOR A DRINK. Late Glenn L. Martin fills gasoline tank of his early pusher from earthenware pitcher before Los Angeles-Catalina Island flight, 1912. Note inner tube life preserver.

appeared destined to stay. Performance figures, even by today's standards, were impressive. By the year's end the altitude record was 13,776 feet, the speed record 82 miles per hour, and the distance record 468 miles. A non-stop flight of 11 hours had been flown and on one epochal half-mile hop a rickety biplane carried 13 people. The most remarkable fact about these flights was that they were all accomplished on planes of less than 100 HP.

That year nearly 45 aeroplanes of different makes were displayed at the third annual Paris Exposition, while in England at least a dozen new manufacturers appeared. In America the Wrights received their first government contract ($125,000.00) for military planes. Other companies sprang up throughout the country like mushrooms. Interest in flying snowballed, and during the year in Britain alone the Royal Aero Club issued 102 new aviator certificates. By the year's end 705 held licenses in France, 192 in England, 144 in Germany and 28 in America.

But flying was far from safe as is attested by the fatality record of 100 deaths by mid-November. Accidents occurred with disturbing regularity. Pilot error, born of a lack of flying knowledge, coupled with faulty structure and poor design contributed largely to this high mortality rate. It is difficult to conceive of a more diabolical combination.

Planes were inherently unstable. The spread between stalling and top speed rarely exceeded 10 miles per hour. A plane capable of flying "hands off" for seconds at a time was a rarity. Few planes, if any, could climb steadily without stalling, compelling their pilots to take them up in "steps," climbing a few feet, then levelling off to recoup lost speed, then climbing again. A plane that could gain 300 feet of altitude a minute was considered exceptional.

Few if any planes could execute climbing turns. In fact, planes banked with the nose down to build up speed. They reacted slowly to the controls because of the leisurely flow of air over their surfaces. By today's standards, they were downright sluggish. Many a pilot failed to become airborne if his engine developed anything less than full power on takeoff, and occasionally some low-powered machines refused to fly at all because of an accumulation of dirt and moisture—the straws that broke the camel's back.

On the ground they were almost unmanageable, particularly those powered by the Gnome rotary engine which had no throttle. Closely spaced wheels contributed to frequent groundloops, and lacking brakes or steerable tailwheels, pilots sat completely at the mercy of their plane's whims. Hard, narrow pneumatic tires and roller bearings on the axles contributed nothing toward reducing their landing roll. Engines failed habitually, especially the Gnomes, unless major-overhauled every few hours. Wings usually succeeded in supporting their own weight on the ground and the plane in the air—but not much more. Mild stalls and dives might be engaged in upon occasions but anything more violent invited disaster.

AERIAL SELF PORTRAIT. British pilot Gordon England snaps his own photograph with camera attached to wing of his seaplane while flying over Brighton, 1913.

INTO THE WILD BLUE YONDER (above). Single place 50 HP Bleriot takes off at Brooklands in 1911, with Gustave Hamel, British pioneer pilot, at controls. Below—1908 production line. Caption under this catalog photo read: "The most up-to-date factory in the world; building motor cars of the air. A scene that may become commonplace: in the workshop of the manufacture of aeroplanes. Those sanguine people who believe that we shall all be flying through the skys (sic) before many years have passed, take encouragement from such scenes as this, a busy time in the workshop of a French constructor of aeroplanes, and argue that such sights will be common before long."

FINAL APPROACH. Bristol 50 HP *Boxkite* floats in over set of barns at edge of flying field in England, 1912. With wing loading of less than two pounds per square foot of area, gliding angle of 40-mile-per-hour biplane was almost completely flat.

BLERIOT COCKPIT (single place version) shows compass to right, map holder amidship, engine revolution counter to right and strange little "cloche" or steering column in middle. Rudder bars not in view. Typical of all planes of its era the Bleriot could not be flown hands off for even seconds at a time. It demanded (and got) constant attention of pilot. Anyone who could fly it could fly anything then in existence.

SPECIAL DELIVERY. 3-cylinder Anzani-powered Bleriot monoplane, workhorse of its day, packed for shipment from factory to owner. Uniformed coachman and smartly groomed horses suggest Bleriot company might well have been prosperous concern.

ADVERTISEMENT in "FLIGHT." By 1909 and 1910 ads of this sort appeared regularly in aviation magazines throughout world. 2,000 miles was a lot of mileage for six days of flying, an accomplishment Farman might well blow its horn about.

CONTACT! Mechanic stands poised to spin Gnome Rotary on 1910 Farman biplane. Surrounded by wires and longerons, working inside cage-like area spinning propeller a good foot *behind* engine, this poor soul took his life in his hands, pilot and passenger seemingly unconcerned at his unhappy lot.

The Aero Bus

With the art of limited flying fairly well established, aeronauts began experimenting with load carrying, for there existed among them an uncontrollable desire to see just how many people their newfangled machines could support.

One of the first to build a plane especially for this purpose was Louis Bleriot who in 1909 had flown the English Channel. His *Aero Bus* appeared in February 1911 at Pau, France, and startled all onlookers by taking off with eight people and flying them about the aerodrome for eight minutes. The pilot and six of his passengers (one of whom was his wife) compressed themselves into the wicker seats that had been designed to hold four, while the eighth person occupied a jump seat far back on the fuselage frame right in front of the vertical stabilizer.

Obviously this flight was merely a stunt, for the plane had not been designed to carry more than four, but it showed what planes could do. For its occupants on that chilly February day, the ride must have been a thriller. The plane was so heavily overloaded and so vastly underpowered (a mere 100 HP) that the takeoff run was torturously slow. One may assume that all eight occupants of the machine were in a jovial, "oh-what-the-hell" mood, and that a good deal of cheering and groaning accompanied the pilot's efforts to get the clumsy rig airborne. Yet, it may also be assumed that many a sigh of relief went up when the Bleriot landed safely.

It was an amazing feat for 1911, and remarkable even by today's standards, for 1911 airfoils were far from efficient, and engines did not always develop their rated power. On this flight the *Bus* wing lifted 5.63 pounds per square foot and developed a power loading of 24.25 pounds per horse power. Compared to a modern Cessna or Piper with an average wing loading of 14 and 15 pounds per square foot and a power loading of 11 or 12, the ship "did all right for itself."

The *Aero Bus* design was modified the following year to carry its passengers in an enclosed cabin —the first passenger-carrying aeroplane to be constructed in which the comfort of its human cargo was taken into serious consideration.

The side entrance body, provided with mica windows for complete visibility below, contained three seats each furnished with a pneumatic cushion to absorb the shock of hard landings. The pilot re-

HIGH DENSITY AIR TRAVEL. With his *Aero Bus,* Louis Bleriot succeeded in making one of his first multi-passenger flights — a remarkable feat considering all handicaps.

...And Aero Taxi

mained out in front, French taxi-cab fashion, but kept in contact with his fares through a speaking tube. His one and only protection from the elements consisted of a novel mica cone suspended in the cross wires of the forward outrigger framework. This device was designed to deflect the wind stream from his face.

Like its predecessor, the *Aero Bus,* the *Aero Taxi* was powered by a 14 cylinder, 100 HP Gnome rotary engine mounted on the trailing edge of the wing, turning a massive 10 foot pusher propeller. Directly in front of the engine rested a carefully streamlined fuel tank.

Its exquisite construction—a characteristic of all Bleriot machines—shows to perfection in the view shown here, taken at the 1911 Paris International Aeronautical Exposition. Note the highly varnished cabin sides, the glove-like fit of the wing fabric, the precision machined tubular shock absorbers, the genuine leather upholstered pilot seat.

But unfortunately the unavailability of engines powerful enough to overcome the extra weight of the cabin and its excessive frontal resistance, doomed the *Aero Taxi's* chance of becoming a profitable carrier long before its first flight, and the aerial voyager continued to ride in the open.

EXPERIMENT IN CABIN COMFORT. Bleriot's '*Aero Taxi*' elegantly furnished but unsuccessful although it flew on several occasions.

START OF WORLD RECORD. Henri Farman carried three men for 1 hour, 2 minutes and 25 seconds on his biplane in 1910.

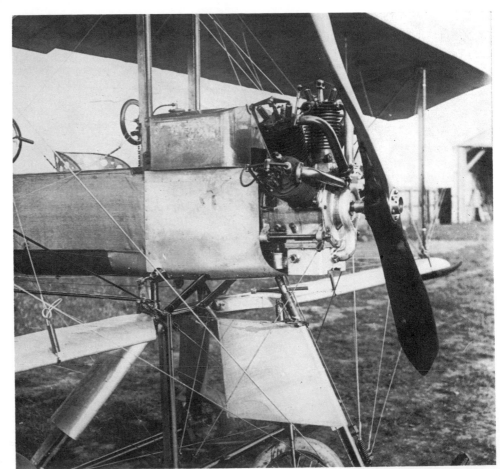

BUSINESS END OF 1911 BREGUET 5 cyl. 60 HP semi-radial engine powered this remarkable biplane with its flexing wings and steerable nose wheel. Fine workmanship and attention to detail is most apparent in this view. Note dual controls.

France Sets Air Records

Henri Farman, English born bicycle rider, auto racer and one of France's aeronautical pioneers, began his celebrated career in French aviation by winning the Grand Prix in 1908 for the first circular flight in Europe. That same year he carried the first passenger, and by March 5, 1910 had carried three for 1 hour 2 minutes and 25 seconds. He is shown here at the completion of this daring accomplishment. Shortly thereafter he carried four, and toward the end of the year broke the world's endurance record with this machine by flying for 8 hours and 12 minutes.

The thought of going aloft today in a contraption such as the 1910 Farman would give the average person a bad case of shivers. By present standards this machine was structurally unsound, incorrectly designed, clumsy, slow to respond and woefully underpowered. And yet in 1910 it was considered to be particularly stable in flight and singularly immune from breakages, and because of this enviable reputation, hardly a machine to fear. So one may draw his own conclusions as to the degree of foolhardiness or bravery these four men showed by their stunt.

Later that same year Louis Breguet took up five passengers and doubled this to ten the next year. Then one of France's great pioneer plane builders and pilots, Roger Sommer, established a world endurance record by remaining aloft for 1 hour and 6 minutes with a total of six people. This feat was accomplished in a Sommer biplane, similar in many respects to the Henri Farman.

LOUIS BREGUET EDGED FARMAN in 1910 by taking these five aloft; a few days later—ten.

SIX FLY FOR OVER AN HOUR (above) and thereby set world's endurance record for pilot Roger Sommer and his Sommer biplane. Passenger accommodations were not ideal, judged by present day standards, but view from seats was superb.

SPORTSMAN PILOT — 1909 VINTAGE — FRANCE about to take off in 2-place Hanriot monoplane.

LAST WORD IN AIRCRAFT.
1911 French Breguet biplane, one of most remarkable planes of the day, possessing such features as tricycle landing gear, steerable nose wheel, all-steel construction, single spar wings. Spar was steel tube around which ribs were made to fit loosely, but were prevented from rotating by means of springs. This design imparted sufficient flexibility to wings to absorb gusts and allow automatic changes in incidence during flight. Lever in cockpit allowed pilot to change incidence at will.

AIRBORNE AND CLIMBING FOR SKY. French aeronaut Louis Paulham streaks off ground at approximately 30 miles per hour in his 50 HP *Henri Farman* biplane in 1910. Any plane possessing forward elevator such as this needed to be flown with great care, for any sudden downward movement of its big surface could trip it as effectively as though landing gear had caught on stone wall. It is not difficult to imagine where unstrapped pilot would go under such circumstances.

PRE-WORLD WAR I SPEED DEMON French pilot Maurice Prevost breaks record at 1913 Gordon-Bennett Aeroplane Race in Rheims, by flying his remarkably clean *Deperdussin* at 124.7 miles per hour. 14 cylinder Gnome rotary engine developing 160 HP gave plane amazing speed.

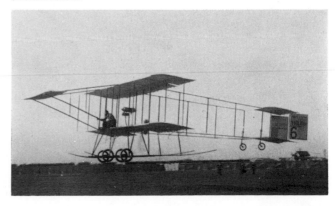

STUNT AT MONACO—1912. With Gnome rotary engine spinning madly, French pilot Fischer prepares to take off his Farman seaplane with three passengers, one behind him and two on floats.

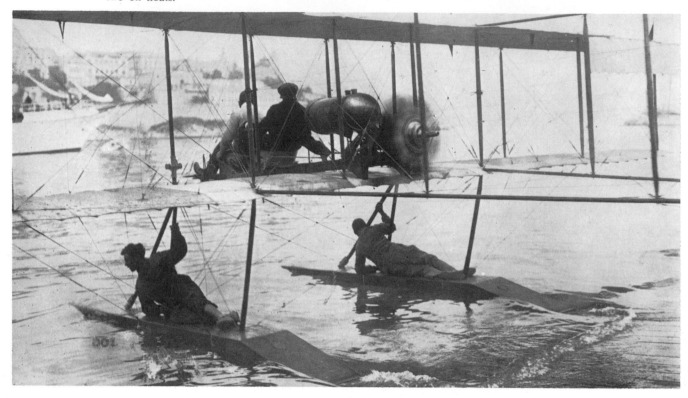

ACCENT ON LANDING GEAR. Planes landed "hot," required sturdy shock-absorbing device on under carriage. One pictured on this French Hanriot of 1910 is typical of the era.

HERE SAT THE PILOT of French Hanriot of 1910 (right) with excellent view of radiator. Lever on left warped wings for lateral control — one on right directed elevators. Air bulb regulated fuel pressure.

Light Plane, 1910 — French Hanriot

The Hanriot, single place monoplane shown on opposite page, like all planes of the day, possessed an elaborate landing gear built to withstand the shock of fast landings on rough fields. Planes of this vintage landed "hot," the spread between stalling and top speed seldom exceeding 15 miles per hour, and very often running as little as two and three miles per hour.

This particular gear consisted of an immensely strong axle mounted in vertical guides on each end, and restrained by four rubber shock cords. The up and down travel in its guides absorbed the bumps of normal landings, but in extremely hard ones, the wheels moved up above the skids, exposing them to the full brunt of the impact. This in turn was transferred to the boat-like fuselage—an extremely strong affair containing pilot's seat, fuel and oil tanks, radiator and the eight cylinder 40 HP E.N.V. engine.

The lever on the left of the pilot's seat warped the wings; that on the right operated the elevators. A pivoted footrest (not visible in the photo on opposite page) controlled the rudder. An ordinary knife switch, taped to the warping lever, turned the ignition on and off and a rubber bulb for maintaining pressure in the fuel tank was attached to the elevator lever. The throttle was located outside of the seat to the left.

SHOW MODEL. Exquisitely finished Bleriot Type *XI* two passenger model displayed at Paris Salon in 1910. Part of fabric and engine compartment cowls were removed to show inner workings.

REMARKABLE IN-FLIGHT PHOTO of 1914 Moreau monoplane. Taken at height of 2,000 feet by camera attached to wing, it shows pilot has taken his hands off controls while passenger (partly hidden behind him) aims gun at flight of birds.

TOP PERFORMER IN 1911. Flimsy-looking Maurice Farman biplane set records impressive even by today's standards. Sept. 2, 1911, it broke world endurance record by remaining aloft 11 hours, later carried useful load of 900 pounds—remarkable achievement for 70 HP. "Flight" commented: "The points that impress themselves upon seeing the machine flying are its rapidity at climbing and its remarkably fine gliding angle. Regarding the former, it has been timed in England recently to climb fully loaded to 1,000 feet inside of five minutes. Some weeks ago in France, Mr. Holt Thomas tells us, one machine climbed to 7,000 feet in twenty-five minutes."

END OF EPOCHAL FLIGHT. French air hero, Roland Garros (in black) upon completion of first over-sea flight in history— a death defying non-stop trip from St. Raphael, France, across the Mediterranean to Bizerte, North Africa — Sept. 23, 1913. 500 mile hop consumed 7 hours and all but 6 quarts of gasoline. To save weight Garros spurned use of pontoons for his fragile 50 HP *Morane-Saulnier* monoplane. For same reason he carried no life preserver, defiantly refused a French Government offer of "stepping stone" escort of ships across sea.

EIGHT HUNDRED FEET WITH 50 HP (above). Willie Haupt's 2-place Bleriot built by American Supply Company of Mineola, N. Y. climbed to 800 feet on its maiden flight and "executed several turns." Power was 50 HP *Roberts* water cooled engine.

EXPERIMENT IN COMMUNICATION — Villacoublay, France, 1911. Wireless telegraph shown set up in Farman biplane, reel antenna to left, headphones amidship and key to right. Radios were exception rather than rule in aircraft even as late as mid-Nineteen Thirties.

ENGLAND

Joy Riding Becomes Big Business

Hendon Airport, on the outskirts of London, became a popular place in early 1913 and 1914. On fair weekends upwards of 20,000 people would flock there and buy tickets for the aerial displays: pylon racing at tree-top level, spot landing contests; acrobatics—steep banks, "vol planes" and occasional loop-the-loops. There were night flights with planes carrying special flares and lights, comic events, record-breaking attempts of various sorts—all manner of spectaculars carried on in a fine, jovial, carnival-like atmosphere.

Passenger-carrying at these meets soon developed into a profitable business as more and more people were tempted by the antics of the airmen to see what it was like to feel air wings. So great became the demand that one of England's great pioneer flyers, Claude Grahame-White was encouraged to build a plane for joy-hopping—the first machine created expressly for this purpose.

This big biplane made its first appearance on the field in September, 1913, and immediately caused a tremendous sensation with the crowd. Designed to carry four passengers and the pilot, it was an outstanding success from the start, and because of its bus-like function soon earned the French name for bus, "Char-A-Banc."

Four wicker seats were placed in the tub-like fuselage which projected far out ahead of the wings. Here the passengers sat in perfect comfort with ample leg room and plenty of space between. The view from either side was completely unobstructed, for this machine had no forward outriggers, and its engine was in the rear.

The pilot sat forward behind a celluloid windshield. Before him was his meagre supply of instruments: an oil pressure gauge, a tachometer compass and air speed indicator. Beside him, on the outside of the fuselage, clung an electric Klaxon which he blew regularly while circling the field in order to attract the attention of the multitudes below. In the rear was the superb 6 cylinder Austro-Daimler engine, probably the most dependable aeroplane motor of the day. Developing 120 HP it was noted for its reliability and smoothness, its ability to idle effortlessly. A most effective muffler silenced the roar of its exhaust, making "Char-A-Banc" an impressively quiet machine in the air.

With a wing loading of less than four pounds per square foot, this machine was extremely stable, and so great was its load-carrying ability that it took off with ease on October 2, 1913 with ten people aboard and flew over Hendon with this mass of humanity for 19 minutes and 47 seconds, thereby setting a British passenger-carrying record that stood for six months.

"Char-A-Banc" continued flying at Hendon until the beginning of World War I brought a halt to Grahame-White's venture in aerial transportation—an undertaking that had introduced flying to many hundreds of people during its short existence.

"ON YOUR MARKS!" GET SET—" (above). Pair of British pilots (probably Morison and Gilmour) await starter's signal as helpers hold back their wide-open *Boxkite's* at start of race in 1910.

"LET GO WHEN HE SIGNALS!" Amount of thrust generated by this *Boxkite's* 50 HP engine is graphically demonstrated by four men holding machine back as pilot runs it up at full throttle. From outbreak of war in 1914, these crude biplanes rendered invaluable service at flying schools at Stonehenge, Brooklands and Eastchurch, England, producing many pilots who later took part in history's first air battles.

WEEKEND AIR MEET IN ENGLAND. Bristol *Boxkite,* flies over sister ship at Hendon, 1910. Speed—40 miles per hour with 50 HP Gnome rotary.

LOW LEVEL PASS AT LAFFANS PLAIN. Every soul but one appears enthralled by the spectacle above.

BRITISH PILOT GUSTAV HAMEL (above) gasses up his Bleriot at Hendcn, May, 1912.

EARLY ENGLISH POWER PLANT. 30 to 60 HP Green here shown in 1910 British Short biplane was one of standbys of the day.

PRIDE OF EARLY WORKMANSHIP. 1911 Bristol *Prier* monoplane reflects skill of builders which far surpassed that of designers. Note enclosed cockpit, spring-loaded nose skids to protect propeller in tail-high landings; main landing gear attached to skids with rubber shock cord; carefully fitted and streamlined landing gear struts. 50 HP Gnome drove plane at 68 miles per hour in still air. Monoplanes of this era developed chronic habit of wing-shedding under certain conditions such as too hasty changes from level flight to nose down attitudes. Such violent maneuvers exerted top loading on upper wing surfaces with sufficient force to snap maze of landing wires as though made of thread. As result popularity of monoplanes waned among aeronauts of the day in favor of more rugged but slower biplanes.

SPORTSMAN PILOT — 1911 VINTAGE—ENGLAND. This cheery chap looked as natty and confident standing beside his 35 HP *Deperdussin* single place monoplane as any modern pilot posing with Cessna *Apache* or *Bonanza*.

50

SAND BAGGED TO DESTRUCTION. In effort to locate weak spots in aircraft structures, manufacturers resorted to crude testing methods. This 1912 British *Coanda* monoplane has been turned upside down, under surface of wings packed with sand bags to simulate flight strains. They show definite signs of bending, only "flying" wires keeping them from snapping off.

BABY BIPLANE. Dual stick made it possible for either occupant to fly this little 1911 Grahame-White *Baby* biplane. Appearance of beautifully built machine is marred only by sloppily tied wires leading from control sticks out to ailerons.

YELLOW PERIL (right). Graceful little two-place monoplane built by Handley Page made 60 miles per hour with its neatly cowled 50 HP Gnome engine.

SKEPTICS SAID "PIGS MIGHT FLY" (lower left) so in 1909 J.T.C. Moore-Brabizon took this porker for an aerial jaunt.

"OFFICE" OF 1911 HANDLEY PAGE MONOPLANE (center). Fine workmanship of this little flyer exhibited at Britain's 1911 Olympia aircraft display is evident in instrumentation, revolution counter, aneroid barometer (for telling height above sea level), searchlight, two gasoline pressure gauges, gasoline pressure pump, wheel, spark and throttle controls on steering column.

PILOT HAD WIDE VISION (right). Frederick Handley Page, pioneer British builder, poses in cockpit of his first plane, *"Blue Bird."* Termed moderately successful, it preceded great HP transports of Nineteen Twenties.

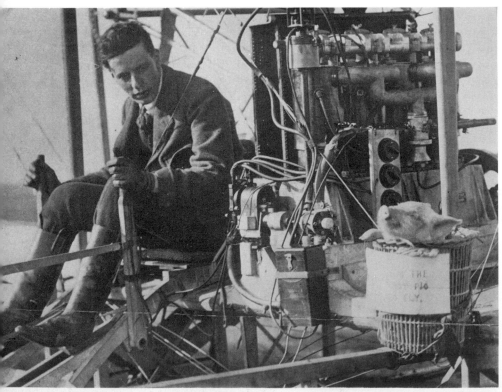

WORLD'S FIRST INHERENTLY STABLE PLANE. This tail-less biplane with sweptback wings first flew at Eastchurch, England, Dec. 20, 1910, and astounded onlookers with its remarkable ability to fly for minutes at a time handsoff, characteristic unknown in any other plane of day. Invented by English Maj. John W. Dunne, machine never became popular although production of few continued for five years. W. Starling Burgess purchased manufacturing rights, building a number in his Marblehead, Mass. factory in 1914 and 1915.

1912 PRODUCTION LINE. Bristol *Boxkite* factory in Filton, England, produced 16 planes in one momentous year, in February, 1911, received order for 8 more from Russian Government.

STEEPLE CHASER OVER HENDON CROWD (above). Pilot Jules Nardini dives his 50 HP *Deperdussin* over admiring onlookers at Fifth London Aviation Meeting, Whitsuntide, May 1913. To left sit two-passenger French Morane-Saulnier powered by 80 HP Gnome and 70 HP Maurice Farman biplane.

FARMAN LONGHORN WAS HISTORIC TYPE used during Aerial Derby at Hendon, England, in 1914 and flown by John Alcock (who flew Atlantic with Brown in 1919), was powered by 8-cyl., water cooled 100 HP *Sunbeam*. Most unique was radiator which stretches around entire fuselage. The *Longhorns* went on to become among first planes to be used by Royal Flying Corps for training purposes during early days of War.

PRIDE OF HENDON AIRPORT (above). Claude Grahame-White's passenger carrying biplane, nicknamed "Char-A-Bank" (French for "bus") about to take off with four passengers. Grahame-White, British "early bird," sits at wheel. Below, he is shown in cockpit of his Bleriot monoplane. He learned to fly in 1909, won the Gordon Bennett air race following year, died in 1959.

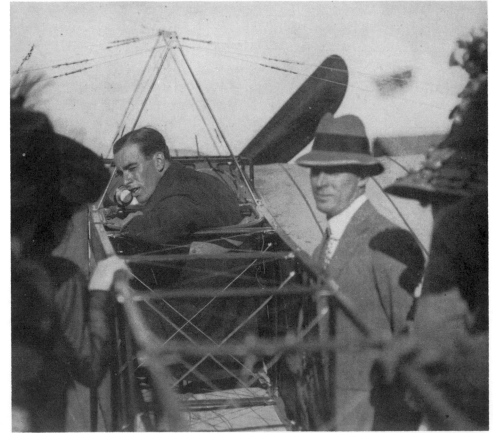

Number 1 Prime Mover of Pre-World War 1 Planes

The famous and peculiar Gnome rotary, an ingenious and beautifully built piece of machinery in which the cylinders were placed around the crankshaft like the spokes of a wheel around the axle. This entire engine revolved, turning the propeller with it at approximately 1200 revolutions per minute. It could not be idled much below 900 to 1000 revolutions, landings and taxiing being accomplished by flicking the ignition switch off and on.

Popular because of its lightness (3 pounds per HP) and its complete freedom from vibration, it proved relatively dependable in spite of such delicate machining that a piston could be smashed between a man's thumb and finger. But it required constant attention. Said one manual:

"When properly assembled and carefully driven, a Gnome engine should run for a total period of 16 hours at full load without requiring any other attention than possible renewal of faulty carbonized spark plugs. After this period the engine must be carefully dismantled and every part carefully examined; defective parts are renewed—not repaired."

(Modern piston engines can be expected to run for well over a thousand hours between major overhauls.) The Gnome cost in the neighborhood of $4000.00 in 1911.

Cowboy of the Air Lanes

COWBOY OF THE AIR LANES. "Col." Samuel F. Cody, American-born cowboy, bronc buster, Wild West Show producer and namesake of the famous "Buffalo Bill"—and the first man to fly an aeroplane in England—is shown above at controls of his 1912 monoplane. One of the most daring and picturesque of all pioneer pilots, Cody repeatedly startled the world with his amazing machines—massive, clumsy biplanes and this remarkable monoplane built expressly to compete in British Military Trials. Extremely fast (83 miles per hour) powered by 120 HP Austro-Daimler engine, weighing 3,100 pounds, it might well have won contest but for a near fatal crackup three weeks before. Landing with dead engine, Cody unavoidably hit a cow grazing on the field, killed the animal and piled the ship into a mass of splinters and Irish linen.

RISKY PERCH FOR TWO. Cody's two place 1910 biplane. Note metal plow seats, rear vision mirror on left strut, tachometer on right. Fine workmanship shows in carefully shaped spars, specially machined ferrules, painstakingly wrapped joints on bamboo members.

PASSENGER ACCOMMODATIONS (above) on "Col." Sam Cody's 1912 biplane. Laughingly called "Orchestral Stalls," these four metal plow seats stacked up in row behind Cody's own perch, carried his son, niece and two helpers on 70 mile an hour jaunt around English countryside. At left, Cody twists his mustache while casting critical eye at his flying competition.

THIRD AERO SHOW at Olympia, England, 1911, indicated general interest in aviation at that time.

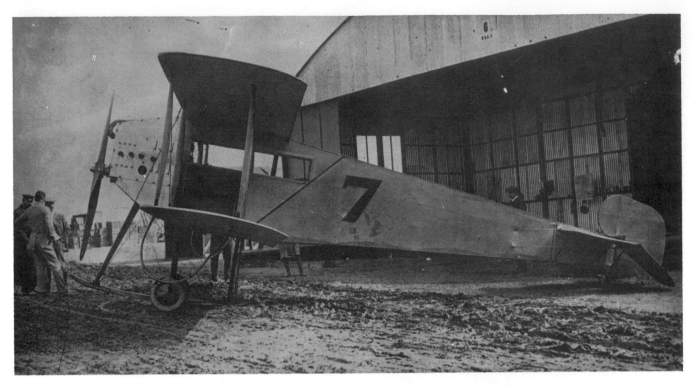

FIRST OF THE CABIN PLANES. Grandpappy of today's enclosed private planes, British-built Avro *Type G* was designed in 1912 by A. V. Roe (shown seated at controls). Although successful, it did not prove popular with pilots long accustomed to sitting in open where they could get "feel" of mounts by flow of air. Twenty-five years elapsed before cabin planes came into vogue.

FLYING FREAK (above). British Valkyrie *Type B*, racing version of three passenger model used in England in 1911 and 1912. This peculiar contraption proved to be exceptionally stable for planes of the day and offered much in way of longitudinal stability, visibility and ultra-safe landing characteristics. With long ski-like skids beneath even dullest student could scarcely fail to land it successfully every time.

THIS WAS FLYING IN 1914 (above). Three passenger plane sporting comfort of enclosed cockpit but lacking protection of any sort for upper half of occupants' torsos. This British Short Brothers biplane, 1913 model, proved exceptionally stable craft, capable of making 58 miles per hour with its 80 HP Gnome. In similar ship equipped with pontoons and driven by new 160 Gnome, English pioneer Francis McClean and two companions flew up the Nile early in 1914. Dogged by usual mechanical difficulties (engine let them down 13 times) they made 1400 mile journey in approximately 11 weeks.

PILOT'S COCKPIT OF VAL-KYRIE (left) disclosed carefully upholstered seat conspicuously lacking in belt (unheard of at time) — equipped with throttle, spark, oiler for 50 HP Gnome rotary engine, ignition switch, rudder bar and joy stick. With this simple instrumentation pilot climbed for altitude, exposed to elements, sitting unstrapped over space, life depending on doubtful strength of maze of wires and struts surrounding him to keep mount from falling apart in mid-air.

RUSSIA

Sikorsky's Four-Engined GRAND

By 1912 two and three hour flights in single-engined aircraft carrying one to three people had become commonplace. More had been carried on occasions to show it could be done and planes with special fuel tanks had stretched the endurance record to 11 or 12 hours. Clipped-wing racing planes, flown by daring pilots, had exceeded 125 miles per hour.

But these were stunts. The average plane of the day did well to carry two people aloft and keep them there for an hour at a speed of 50 to 60 miles per hour. Engines of the day were provokingly undependable and produced scarcely enough power to drag the clumsy, unstreamlined machines through the air.

Obviously this sort of mediocre performance could not continue if aviation were to survive but the question of how to improve it was not an easy one to answer. One solution seemed to lie in the use of a number of engines, for this would add the needed power and at the same time provide some sort of safety factor. But more engines meant more weight which in turn meant a larger wing which in itself added more weight, and the circle became vicious.

Early in 1913 the multi-engine barrier was cracked by Igor Sikorsky, then a budding engineer in Petrograd. In May of that year he successfully flew the *Grand,* the world's first four-engined plane. This huge biplane with a wing spread of 92 feet, weighed 9000 pounds. Four 100 HP water-cooled *Argus* engines arranged in tandem on the wings gave it a speed of 60 miles per hour.

The glass-enclosed cabin—tall enough for a man to stand upright in—was the first ever seen on an airplane. Inside were seats for four, a bench and a table, and in the rear—a small washroom. The pilot sat forward, and beside him a co-pilot, possibly the first ever carried on a plane. Engine and blind flying instruments were arranged on the dash board before them.

Nothing like the *Grand* had ever been seen before, and no one besides its creator believed it could possibly fly. It was argued that if one engine should stop, it would become unmanageable, that it was too clumsy to land; that it could not be controlled from a closed cabin. But in spite of their predictions, the machine flew well, even with one engine throttled back, and more than fifty successful flights were made with it before it was abandoned and a bigger and better ship constructed.

Somewhat heavier and larger than the *Grand, Ilia Mourometz* outperformed it with bigger engines, two developing 140 HP, and two 125 HP. This machine boasted a small sleeping compartment as well as the passenger cabin and wash room, and as an added luxury—electric lights and heat. With twelve people aboard, this amazing ship once succeeded in climbing to 6900 feet, remaining airborne for over six hours. And on another flight it broke a world record by carrying 16 passengers. (It is interesting to note that both *Grand* and *Ilia Mourometz* sported open air balconies on which passengers could walk during flight—a supreme thrill completely denied modern day aerial travelers.)

Although there was much room for improvement, these 4-engined craft, built only ten years after the Wright Brothers' faltering 12-second hop, were practical and entirely capable of transporting passengers and freight on scheduled runs. And but for World War 1, aerial transportation in luxurious 4-engined planes might well have begun right then and there on a grand scale.

GRAND CRACKED MULTI-ENGINED BARRIER (top opposite). In May, 1913, over Petrograd, young engineer Igor Sikorsky successfully flew this huge biplane—world's first four-engined aircraft. It had wing spread of 92 feet, weighed 9,000 pounds. (Bottom) Emperor Nicholas II inspects *Grand* from forward balcony with Sikorsky, (extreme right) July, 1913.

INTERIOR OF SIKORSKY GRAND showing pilot's compartment with dual controls, electric light, curtains, benches and part of passenger quarters.

ILIA MOUROMETZ **LANDS AT PETROGRAD (above).**
Ski-equipped, this big biplane floats toward snow-covered
airport while two of its passengers watch from upper platform—Feb. 1914.

TWO EARLY AMERICAN AERONAUTS (below). Adolph
and Charles Witteman, Staten Island brothers, seated at
controls of their 1909 75 HP Whitehead-powered biplane.

AND IN THE UNITED STATES

SPOT LANDING CONTEST—1910. Wright *Model B* approaches line during week-long International Aviation Meet at Belmont Park, Long Island, N. Y.—most important aerial event the country had ever seen. Attended by thousands including America's top society, meet attracted the world's most skilled airmen: Orville Wright, Claude Grahame-White, Walter Brookins, Arch Hoxsey, Roland Garros, Hubert Latham and many others. The use of landing skids on Wright planes gave them tremendous advantage over conventional wheeled machines. Not only did they drag the planes to a stop in a fraction of the distance but they eliminated the need for heavy, complicated, shock-absorbing landing gears that characterized all other makes.

WORLD'S FIRST CLIP WING RACER? Wilbur Wright (in black derby) at Belmont Park, 1910, stands in slipstream of his Wright *Model R* "Baby Grand" while brother Orville (between nose wheels) observes engine before climbing aboard. With span of only 21 feet and wing area of 140 square feet, it attained speed of between 70 and 80 miles per hour with 60 HP engine. Pilot sat close to engine, left arm wrapped around nearest strut for support.

ROBERTS ENGINE

SPORTSMAN PILOT — 1910 VINTAGE—AMERICA. Henry W. Walden, New York aeronaut, and his *Walden III* — America's first monoplane.

EARLY AMERICAN POWER PLANT—1912. 50 HP *Roberts* engine was used with considerable success in many early U.S. planes. Similarity between it and standard marine motors of the day is most obvious.

GLENN L. MARTIN'S FLYING YACHT. Powered by 80 HP Curtiss V-8 engine, 4-place hydroplane performed well, flying at top speed of about 60 miles per hour. Motor was cooled by pair of Hall Scott radiators set parallel to slipstream clear of pilot's vision. Two Martin-designed mufflers effectively silenced engine, a weight concession Martin accepted in interest of quiet flight.

FIRST LETTER WRITTEN by an American pilot in the air, it is believed. Shakiness of writing is due to vibration of motor. **(Extreme left)**

ARCH HOXSEY — AMERICAN IMMORTAL pilot of pioneer days stands on shoulders of student pilot as he pours water into radiator of his Wright *B* pusher about 1910. On Dec. 23, 1910, Hoxsey set a world altitude record of 11,474 feet, flight taking 2 hours 15 minutes to complete.

SPERRY DEMONSTRATES HIS AUTO-PILOT (above). By 1914 French War Department, already deep in aviation experiments, offered a prize of 50,000 francs for a "stable airplane." Over 80 competitors from all over the world participated but prize went to an American, Lawrence Sperry, who had been experimenting for two years with a "gyro-stabilizer." Sperry put on a most convincing demonstration by flying over Paris standing in his cockpit while companion calmly walked along wings. Although sparingly used by planes during formative years of aviation, automatic pilot is standard equipment on virtually every commercial passenger plane used today.

AMERICAN FLYBOY—1911 (above). Frank Fitzsimmons at controls of Henry Walden's *Walden XI*, all-American monoplane. This was tremendously rugged airplane for its day, constructed largely of shelby steel tube filled with second-growth hickory for extra strength. Longerons consisted of straight grain ash, laminations spruce, propeller laminated mahogany, wings covered with Irish linen. 4-cyl. Hall Scott water-cooled engine drove machine close to 60 miles per hour.

FIRST SPERRY GYRO AUTOMATIC PILOT installed in Curtiss Model E Hydroplane in 1912. Pilot is C. K. "Doc" Wildman, Curtiss Hydro instructor, Hammondsport, N.Y. Wildman was Lawrence Sperry's instructor at Curtiss Flying Schools, San Diego. Square plate on radiator is air speed control.

TO EMPHASIZE GREAT SPEED of planes daring pilots often raced automobiles and boats
—1915. Above, Raymond V. Morris, Curtiss Company manager in California, races 90 HP
speedboat. Below, De Lloyd Thompson races Barney Oldfield. Morris is flying Curtiss flying
boat while Thompson pilots 90 HP Gyro-*Duplex* Day tractor biplane.

AN AEROPLANE VIEW OF TARRYTOWN. Photo taken by Mr. Fausto Rodriguez from the Thomas flying boat.

AERIAL SIGHTSEERS. During May 1914 pilot Ralph Brown (shown here at wheel of his Thomas flying boat) carried over 100 passengers at Dobb's Ferry, N. Y.

Tampa to St. Pete in Twenty Minutes

The World's first scheduled airline began operations on January 1, 1914, flying between St. Petersburg and Tampa, Florida. A lone Benoist flying boat piloted by Anthony (Tony) Janus, one of the country's more famous pioneer pilots, was used on the run and made two round trips a day carrying one passenger at a time.

The 22 mile flight was made in an average of 20 minutes, and the fare was $5.00 for a passenger and his baggage. Fat men of over 200 pounds were obliged to pay extra fare.

The operation was not a financial success, and after a few months the line ceased operations. But it had proved that passenger carrying by air was feasible and safe, and it provided an insight of things to come in the field of aerial transportation.

BENOIST TYPE XIV SEAPLANE in flight with four people aboard. Roger Janus is pilot, at his right Hugh Robinson—behind are Elmer Straub and Russell Froelich of St. Louis Globe Democrat. Photo was made in 1916 while in flight by means of camera attached to outer wing strut.

BENOIST COULD CARRY SIX. Ship was driven by pair of Roberts 100 HP water cooled engines. Note cutouts in upper wing surfaces over each engine.

ST. PETERSBURG-TAMPA AIRBOAT LINE—1914. Tony Janus starts on first trip, leaving St. Pete, while hundreds watch from shore.

FLORIDA AIRBOAT LINE—1914 (above). Tony Janus appears fourth from left beside the Benoist airboat at inauguration ceremonies. Plane made two trips a day, covered the twenty-two mile run in twenty minutes. Below, Tony Janus and unidentified passenger ready for flight on Florida Airboat Line. Fare was $5 if you weighed under 200 pounds.

FIVE HAD FAITH. Four passengers about to take off in American-built 90 HP Christofferson tractor biplane in 1915. Although obviously a publicity stunt, it showed load carrying ability of frail-looking machine.

IN-FLIGHT VIEW OF BENOIST AIRBOAT carrying passenger between Tampa and St. Petersburg, 1914. Note American flags and pennants streaming from wing struts.

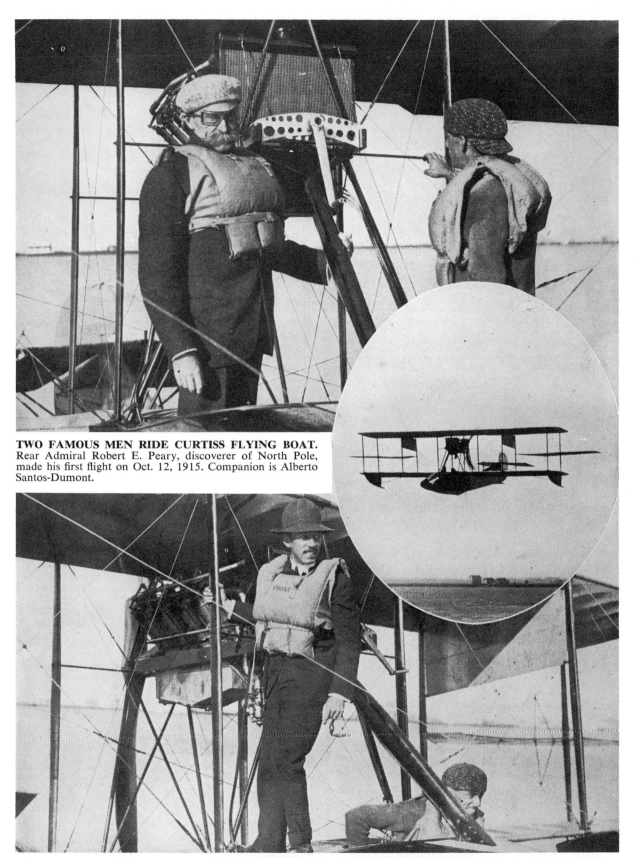

TWO FAMOUS MEN RIDE CURTISS FLYING BOAT.
Rear Admiral Robert E. Peary, discoverer of North Pole, made his first flight on Oct. 12, 1915. Companion is Alberto Santos-Dumont.

ALBERTO SANTOS-DUMONT, first man to fly a heavier-than-air machine in Europe about to embark on his first plane trip on American continent—Long Beach, Long Island, N.Y.

Freaks and Fizzles

EXPERIMENT THAT FAILED. Alberto Santos-Dumont's *Demoiselle,* world's first light plane, shown garbed in twin props. Exasperated at having broken this plane's single propeller after 200 yard hop in 1908, Santos-Dumont (first man to fly in Europe) replaced it with this pair of old style cloth-covered paddles, cooling engine with three blader direct-coupled to it. Contraption failed to fly (naturally) although *Demoiselle* proved amazingly able with single prop on later flights.

FRENCH EXPERIMENT that didn't prove out. 1910 twin propellered monoplane representing effort to spread more airflow over greater wing area. *Liore* was equipped with steerable tail wheel, great innovation for 1910.

DAVIDSON'S "GYROPTER" or ROTARY WING FLYING MACHINE.

If you want to make money, and at the same time help towards "British Supremacy of the Air," send along your contribution to the expense of the construction of the "GYROPTER" Flying Machine. Don't whine about other countries getting the better of us, and at the same time button up your pocket. You know we as a country will have to pay pretty heavily later on if the public do not contribute NOW, and you personally will miss the profits.

Upwards of £15,000 has been expended by Mr. Davidson on his experiments during the last 20 years.

The construction of the present machine which is fast approaching completion, has cost £6,000 during the past year. A few thousands are still required to complete.

Five fully-paid shares in the Davidson's Gyropter Flying Machine Ltd., will be given for every £5 now contributed.

The Syndicate (owning the entire right, title, and interest in the invention, which will as soon as success is attained, be sold to a larger Company at a big profit), is divided into 60,000 shares, all issued and fully paid, ranking equally. 30,000 of these will be distributed amongst those who have rendered services, and in the proportion of Ten shares for every £10 contributed in cash during the past or now.

The Machine at present being constructed (see illustration) will be capable of travelling with automatic stability, at a speed of upwards of 200 miles per hour, carrying from 20 to 30 passengers with greater safety than by rail.

The satisfactory completion of this machine is a matter of National importance, and it is hoped that the public will generously contribute; especially as each contributor will share in the profits of success, and otherwise participate proportionately in privileges and preferences which will not be accorded to those who do not now contribute.

Mr. Davidson is willing to show the machine during construction to British subjects who have *bona fide* intention of contributing when they are satisfied that the undertaking deserves their support, but an appointment must be made by intending visitors.

The works are at Amerden Bank, Taplow, about 200 yards below Bray Lock, on the River Thames, just over a mile from Taplow Station by road.
TELEPHONE 338 MAIDENHEAD, A THREEPENNY TRUNK CALL FROM LONDON.
Contributions should be made payable, and addressed to GEORGE L. O. DAVIDSON, or Col. LEWIS HALL, C.B., Amerden Bank, Taplow.

To G. L. O. DAVIDSON, Amerden Bank, Taplow.

Dear Sir, Date..
Enclosed I beg to hand you cheque for £.................. ....as a contribution towards the construction of your "Gyropter" Flying Machine, the receipt of which please acknowledge.

Yours truly, Signature...
Address.......... ....
....

AERIAL CON GAME. With flying attaining popularity, the day experienced its full share of crackpots and promoters. This advertisement appearing in 1910 issue of "Flight" typified the sort of thing foisted on public.

SOME DAYS IT DOESN'T PAY TO GO UP. French pilot Legel came a cropper when his biplane hit a telephone pole in 1911.

BUILDER DIDN'T LAUGH at *De Pischoff,* French monoplane with automobile-like fuselage. First designed in Austria, was later developed in France. Carried two at 48 miles per hour, cost 25,000 francs.

FOWLER TRACTOR, its V-8 Hall Scott engine resting in open on pair of two-by-fours, radiator effectively blocking forward vision, flew across Panamanian Isthmus in 1913 carrying motion picture cameraman.

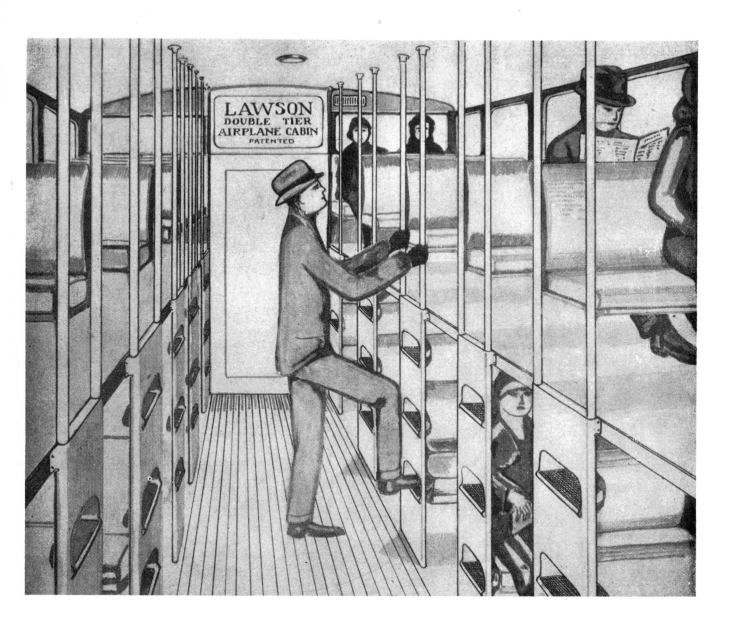

SCHEME THAT NEVER MATERIALIZED. 12-engined super air liner seating 100—dream of Alfred W. Lawson, pioneer designer, who claimed its high density seating arrangement would make it more profitable passenger carrier than railroad train. Construction of such a machine presented too many engineering problems in 1927 and it was never built.

STRANGE FORERUNNER OF PLANES TO COME. 1908 French Antoinette monoplane with single wheel landing gear and powered by V-8 50 HP Antoinette engine. This engine (also made in 16 cyl. size developing 100 HP) was favorite with European pilots until superseded by Gnome rotary in 1909 and powered Santos-Dumont's plane on its premier European flight in 1906. Note pipe radiator extending along right side of fuselage.

POWER PACK — 1911 STYLE (left). 60 HP 5 cyl. R.E.P. engine designed and built by Frenchman Robert Esnault-Pelterie clings to front of his single-place monoplane. Speed of machine was claimed to be 70 miles per hour with endurance of 2½ hours, claim that might be taken with grain of salt. Note shock-absorbing device on landing gear.

SEAT IN CLOVER (below). Pilot compartment of 1910 Fritz monoplane slung in landing gear provided minimum protection to occupant. Left wheel controlled lateral stability—right wheel, vertical. Foot-operated pedals directed rudder.

AFTER THE WAR WAS OVER

WITH the advent of World War 1, private and commercial flying ceased in Europe as its industries concentrated entirely on the development of war materials.

From the beginning it appeared that aviation would play a vital part, for aircraft possessed advantages hitherto unknown in military operations. They could fly above the enemy, spy down upon him and drop bombs on him. The need for great masses of bombers and observation planes and fighters to protect them sprang up over night.

But the story of military aviation and its part in war has no place in this book. It is purposely omitted, for little similarity exists between civil and military aircraft. Each is designed for a particular purpose. Neither can be used efficiently in the role of the other. Their stories do not overlap.

With the end of World War 1, the great aircraft factories in Europe and America, which had been turning out planes in droves, suddenly found themselves with cancelled orders and partially completed work on hand. Their plight was a desperate one, and in an effort to remain in business, and to make the most of a poor thing, many of them turned to the conversion of military aeroplanes for commercial use.

Tremendous advancements in airplane design had been made during the war years, but they were entirely of a military nature. Nothing had been done to develop transport planes of any sort, and by the time the Armistice was signed on Nov. 11, 1918, not a single machine capable of carrying passengers in anything but the most primitive fashion existed.

Interest in flying had reached tremendous proportions during the war by a civilian population intrigued by the daring exploits of allied and enemy airmen. Just how many of these people could be counted upon to fly, given the opportunity, was a big question to which no one had the answer. But for desperate manufacturers it was a question with hope, and many became convinced that commercial aviation held a great and prosperous future.

A few enterprising pioneers, confident that the public would soon beat a path to their doors, formed airlines and charter organizations, using the least unsuitable of the many types of planes then available in the surplus market. Some lent themselves grudgingly to modifications. Some were complete failures. All were makeshift. They were not always comfortable, and they certainly were far from economical to operate, but they filled a gap until something better could be developed.

PAY LOAD TO PARIS in two passenger *DH-4* powered by Rolls Royce 350 HP engine. This was initial flight by S. Instone & Co. Ltd. from Hounslow, England, Oct. 13, 1919.

Britain Spans The Channel

One of the first planes to enter scheduled service in Europe after the war was an Aircraft Transport & Travel Ltd. *DH-9B* which left Croyden Airport near London for Paris on August 25, 1919.

The *DH-9B* was a standard allied *DH-9* day bomber refined for passenger carrying by the removal of its Lewis gun in the rear observer's cockpit and the substitution of a seat for two. Here sat the passengers, squeezed in like sardines, attired in full flying regalia: helmets, goggles, flying suits and boots. Flying in 1919 could be exceedingly uncomfortable at times, and yet people willingly paid a hundred dollars for the trans-Channel crossing, a fact which encouraged operators to order more and larger planes.

The *DH-16*, a far more carefully modified version of the *DH-9*, proved superior to the *DH-9B*. It packed a hundred and forty five more horse power and it sported a 4-place passenger cabin with windows, a folding top, and a heater.

Access to this cramped little area was through the top, and the loading and unloading developed into something of an art. Passengers climbed a 3-step metal ladder on the side of the fuselage up and over the coaming and down into the cockpit onto the four seats, a procedure that must have been particularly unpleasant for women with their ankle-length skirts and many petticoats.

CLEARED FOR TAKEOFF. Passenger cabin of DeHaviland *DH-16* held four people if not too large, comfortably if they didn't move. Top folded up for exit and entrance. Over 150 of these rugged old planes saw service on world's embryo airways.

SIXTEEN GO ALOFT AT ONCE. This laughing group packed itself into narrow confines of Curtiss H-7 flying boat for aerial jaunt. Closeness of propellers to part of human cargo made flight particularly hazardous.

Once the human cargo became settled—two facing forward and two aft—the metal top closed down on them like a coffin lid, and there they remained, cramped and immobile until the plane landed. The roar of the engine and general rattling and vibration of the machine itself was so severe that communication was utterly impossible and limited entirely to sign language and notes.

The pilot sat forward under the top wing in an open cockpit immediately behind the thundering 12-cylindered Rolls Royce *Eagle*. Completely divorced from his passengers and probably quite oblivious of them, his efforts must have been directed solely toward flying his big machine and navigating it in the fog and poor visibility that characterized the Channel area.

DeHaviland reconditioned and remodeled over 150 of these *DH-9s,* providing it with its bread and butter for some time during the lean post-war years.

This company also formed the DeHaviland Aeroplane Hire Service, and developed it into a profitable venture with nearly a dozen *DH-9Cs.*

By March 1920, Aircraft Transport & Travel Ltd. had grown to the point of having 16 pilots on its payroll, a few *DH-9As,* one *DH-18* and a *DH-34.* In August still another outfit, Daimler Air Lines commenced business between London and Paris with a fleet of new *DH-34s.*

The *34* was an eminently satisfactory machine. Its eight place cabin, big and roomy enough for the passengers to get up and move about in, boasted the comfort of a toilet and the service of a cabin boy. Its 450 HP Napier *Lion* proved immensely dependable although barely powerful enough for such a large machine. Takeoffs occasionally became touch and go affairs especially in muddy ground under full load conditions. But it served its purpose well and in all DeHaviland built twelve.

AIRLINE CAPTAIN—1919 VERSION (above left). At start of London-Paris daily service Pilot H. Shaw poses for picture as passenger backs his way into narrow confines of *DH-16*'s cabin. At right, three women passengers peer from curtained splendor of *DH-16*. Early designers apparently felt curtains and vases achieved a tranquilizing effect on passengers, for virtually every cabin plane contained either or both. They also provided a homelike touch with minimum weight.

FIRST PLANE OF OLDEST AIRLINE (below left). KLM's semi-converted De Haviland *DH-9* embarking at Amsterdam for London in 1920. At right is cheery aviator who flew the cross-Channel route in 1919.

Public Demanded Size, Speed, Comfort

Making a strong bid for passenger carrying business in 1920 was the Bristol *Pullman,* a 4-engined triplane manufactured by Bristol Aircraft Corp.

Its prototype was the *Braemar,* a bomber ordered by the Air Board but completed too late to see service in the War. The transformation from a war machine to a civilian transport consisted of increasing the width and depth of the fuselage, and fitting out the interior to accommodate 14 passengers.

No effort was spared to make this plane attractive and comfortable, and the cabin was luxurious even by today's standards. The color scheme was pleasant; the upholstery superb; attractive curtains hung at each window; each seat had its own foot warmer and (as an added comforting touch) a basin for use in case of air sickness.

Two large fuel tanks in the forward part of the fuselage divided the cabin into two compartments, the forward one seating six and the rear one eight. The two were united by a narrow passageway between the tanks.

The pilot and co-pilot sat forward, their cockpit completely enclosed. This feature was not popular with pilots who had grown used to sitting in the open where they could tell from the rush of air on their cheeks whether they were slipping or crabbing or flying straight. Only in the open could they hear the sounds of the wind in the wires—the sounds that told them so accurately whether they were climbing or diving. None of these natural aids could be used by the pilot of the Pullman who was forced to sit in a sealed compartment.

But the enclosed fuselage was aerodynamically more efficient than the open type and the *Pullman's* performance was exceptional as a result: speed 135 miles per hour; landing speed 55; climb to 5000′ in six minutes. And the pilots soon found they could fly as well sitting indoors as out.

To meet a demand for a medium sized plane capable of carrying a handful of passengers on domestic short haul routes, Bristol designed and built the *Ten Seater.* It first flew on January 18, 1924, and later that year joined the newly formed Imperial Airways' fleet of transports.

FOR SHORT HAULS IN BRITAIN, Bristol Aircraft designed the *Ten-Seater.* Its first flight on Jan. 18, 1924 led to service with newly formed Imperial Airway's fleet of transport planes.

The Great Handley Pages

Among the more outstanding passenger plane conversions developed during this early period was the Handley Page *0/700,* the civilian version of the famous *0/400* bomber.

This passenger machine, seating ten in its comfortable wicker chairs, first went into operation on Handley Page Transport Ltd.'s line in August of 1919 flying between Cricklewood airdrome and Paris. Daily flights were offered in each direction.

The following year Amsterdam was included in the daily service and by the end of the year an efficiency of 76% for the London-Paris run and 86% for the London-Amsterdam route had been chalked up—an amazing record for a pioneer operation such as this.

That year Handley Page introduced the *W/8,* a larger, and more efficient twin engined biplane capable of carrying 12 passengers in the greatest degree of comfort so far known. This machine had won the

Air Ministry's civil aviation competition and later on at Brussels it was awarded first prize for large passenger planes. For years this big biplane held the world's weight lifting record.

Used to a lesser degree, but still deserving mention here because of its massiveness and its great load carrying ability, was the *V/1500.* Originally built to bomb Berlin, this four-engined giant could carry a useful load of 6½ tons. Its wing spread was 126 feet, 9 feet more than a Douglas *DC-6,* and fully loaded it weighed 13½ tons. Its four 350 HP V-12 Rolls Royce *Eagle* engines produced a top speed of 100 miles per hour.

As a transport plane it carried 30 passengers—40 in a pinch—with a cruising radius approaching 12 hours. But it was too large, and far too costly to operate for commercial work, and Handley Page used it sparingly.

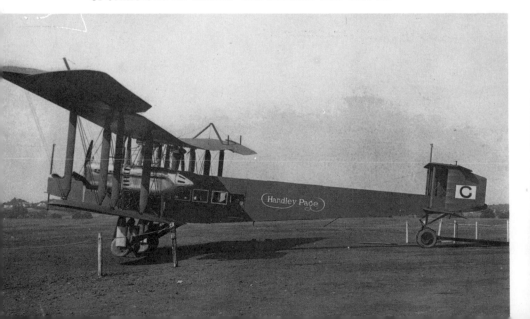

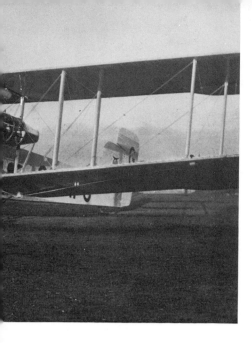

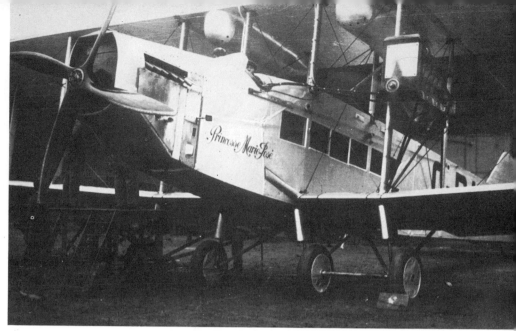

CHECK OUT (top left). Flight and ground crews of Handley Page *W-400* appear cheerful as its two Rolls Royce 360 HP engines warm up. Port propeller can be seen in extreme right part of photo.

HANDLEY PAGE WINS PRIZE (top center). Carrying 12 in new comfort, this twin-engined ex-bomber won Air Ministry competition first prize at Brussels for large passenger planes.

AFRICAN PRINCESS (top right). 3-engined Handley-Page *Hamilton* airliner used by Belgium's S.A.B.E.N.A. in Congo service. This 1924 plane, capable of carrying dozen passengers at 103 miles per hour, is shown being checked over before flight. Port Napier *Lion* revs up while mechanics examine starboard engine. Four-blade, wooden propellers were used on all three engines.

FAMOUS HANDLEY PAGE 0-700 (below left).

ALL ABOARD FOR FRANCE (below center). Handley Page *W-8B*, owned by Handley Page Transport Ltd., loads passengers at London Airport for Paris, June 1923.

UNGAINLY-LOOKING *W-8B* TAKES OFF FOR EUROPE (below right). One of Handley Page's 14-passenger transports lumbers into air, engines pulling madly against vast resistance of unstreamlined landing gear, struts, wires and wing surfaces.

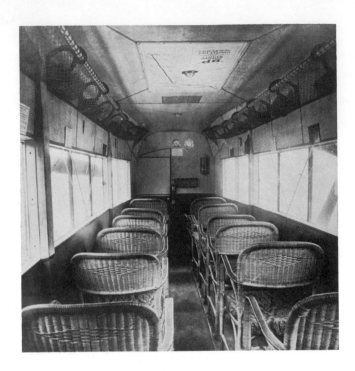

SUMPTUOUS INTERIORS (above). Handley Page *W-10* offered its 14 passengers superb vision from big sliding windows, the privilege of strolling forward to stretch and look at altimeter and speedometer on bulkhead, overhead map of dog-leg course between London and Paris. Yet these big ships with low wing loadings (sometimes not over 5 pounds were lifted per square foot of wing surface) could be extremely uncomfortable in rough air. They offered an amazing safety however, for their slow landing speeds—50 to 55 miles per hour) took most of danger out of forced landings. Below, interior of *W-8*. Note candelabra.

OUT OF LONDON FOG FLIES PROGRESS. Imperial Airways *Argosy* arrives from Paris. Arrival of an airliner in 1924 was a sight to behold.

BOMBER GOES COMMERCIAL. Completed too late for war duty, this big 4-engined triplane was Bristol Aircraft's bid for transport service. It carried 14 passengers in sumptuous accommodations at 135 miles per hour.

The Passenger Was King

Biplanes sat close to the ground because their propeller arcs did not extend below their lower wings. For this reason, loading passengers presented no problems. A two or three-step ladder did the trick. With the advent of low-wing monoplanes with wing-mounted engines and large diameter propellers, landing gears became longer-legged and so did the loading ramps.

From a passenger point of view, the most unpleasant feature of these early planes was noise. The roar of engine exhausts thundered through the thin fabric sides setting up such a clatter in the cabin that conversation became a real hardship, and in some cases an impossibility. And adding to this clamor was the howl of the reduction gears and propellers, the slapping of fabric, the scream of the wind forcing its way through the maze of struts and wires between the wings.

Sound insulation did not exist. Neither did mufflers. In an attempt to dump the roar behind, engineers occasionally extended the pipes back beyond the cabin, as shown in photos, pages 88-89. But this resulted in only a slight drop in the decibel count.

In the *DH-9s,* the French Spads and Potez, occupants communicated solely by notes. It was useless to shout. No one could hear a thing. Yells could be understood on the Handley Pages and the *Goliaths,* and on the Fokker *11* and *111,* passengers could make themselves understood by screaming at each other—provided the windows were closed.

But noise was only one of the discomforts of early flying. Vibration, especially on planes with nose engines, was decidedly irritating, shaking the occupants and setting up all sorts of unpleasant rattles. Ventilation, provided through opening windows, worked well in summer, but proved a dismal failure in winter. And because planes of the day lacked heating systems, passengers could do little in cold weather but sit and shiver in the stuffy atmosphere.

Most planes of the day were equipped with wicker chairs, the lightest furniture available. Lack of space prevented use of reclining seats, thus compelling passengers to sit bolt upright for hours on end, although in the multi-engined machines they could at least walk around and stretch their legs.

Most transports contained toilet facilities, albeit cramped and primitive. Few planes carried food or drink, and on most, smoking was not permitted.

In an effort to provide an air of dignity and solidity to these makeshift planes, designers created ornate interiors. But these contributed nothing to bodily comfort, simply adding weight to already overloaded, underpowered machines.

Many carried notices regarding the safety of flight, urging passengers to relax and take it easy. One in the Fokker *11* read in three languages: "The pilot of this machine has been selected after long training. He knows his business. Trust him and don't worry." Others warned occupants not to throw objects from the windows. Some provided maps so travelers could trace their course while in flight—a particularly fascinating pastime on the *Goliath* from its "bayview" window in front. Still others supplied booklets describing the sensations of flight and offering calming advice on bumps which it compared to waves on the sea, and which it urged the passenger to ignore. It is interesting to observe that this sort of propaganda, designed to sooth nervous travelers, has continued in use on practically all airliners to the present day.

Three Engines Make History

In March 1924, the four independent airlines that had been operating in England since 1919 and struggling for survival since 1922, joined under the name of Imperial Airways, Ltd., a State-financed enterprise.

Handley Page aircraft dominated 90 percent of the flying with the old *0/700s, W/8bs* and the *W/10.* But in 1926 a newcomer entered the field.

Sir W. G. Armstrong-Whitworth Ltd., which had previously built fighters, introduced the *Argosy,* a trimotored biplane that carried 20 passengers, their baggage and a crew of two.

Three air cooled Armstrong Siddeley *Jaguar* engines producing a total of 1100 HP gave it a top speed of 110 miles per hour, and a cruising speed of 90. Altitude could be maintained on any two.

The passenger cabin was 29 feet long and 4½ feet wide with seats arranged on each side of the aisle, each with its own window that could be opened or closed in flight to suit the occupant's fancy. The cabins were equipped with baggage racks, electric lights, hot air heaters and toilet accommodations. The pilots sat forward in an open cockpit directly behind the middle engine, a remarkably unstreamlined piece of machinery bearing all the earmarks of having been tacked on the nose as an afterthought.

Occasionally a steward was carried to serve light lunches and drinks while in flight, although his pres-

PRE-FLIGHT PHOTO (below left). Group of passengers and crew members pose before flight in Handley Page *V/1500.* One of these 4-engined giants carried 40 people over London in 1919, had useful load capacity of 6½ tons.

ence and his provisions meant cutting the passenger capacity to eighteen. Sending and receiving radio was a part of the plane's standard equipment.

The *Argosies* of the *City of Glasgow* class flew mainly the *Silver Wing* and the afternoon *DeLuxe* London-Paris run, and operated without interruption until 1933. Somewhat more powerful models were used on the London-Karachi-Delhi route and on the run from London to Capetown.

THE CAIRO-BAGHDAD EXPRESS

De Haviland built the *DH-66 Hercules* in 1926 for Imperial Airways' Indian routes between Cairo and Baghdad—the first line in the Empire air chain.

Vast stretches of desert and waste lands dictated the basic requirement for a safe airplane: an ample safety margin in the event of engine failure. The *Hercules* met the requirement with its ability to fly with one engine out.

De Haviland, in typical British fashion of the day, made little or no attempt at streamlining. Lack of engine and landing gear fairing, the free-swivelling tail wheel cocked at a 45 degree angle, exposed control wires, pipes and vents on the fuel tanks; the wind scoops, oil coolers, the passenger ladder—all stole miles from the plane's speed. A removable coupe top over the cockpit, protected the pilot and co-pilot from the hot sun during the dry season.

Three 500 HP *Jupiters* gave the *Hercules* a top speed of 130 miles per hour and a cruising speed of 110. It weighed 15,600 pounds all up, and carried 12 passengers and their baggage. In all, 11 were built and used by Imperial with great success for many years.

GREAT FOUR-ENGINE *HANNIBAL HP42*

Throughout the 1930s, giant Handley Page biplanes of the *Heracles* and *Hannibal* class spanned the English Channel on regular and frequent daily flights. Lumbering and slow, these were the first four-engined transport planes ever used in scheduled service in the world. And they were the safest and most comfortable.

Handley Page built eight of these monstrous *42s* for Imperial Airways in two forms: the Eastern, used on the tropical African run—Karachi, Cairo, Kisumu, Capetown; and the Western, designed for the short haul Paris-London route.

The eight were identical except for seating arrangement, the Western carrying 40 passengers; the Eastern somewhat less to allow more room for cargo and mail for the provinces.

No re-worked military plane, the *HP-42* was designed from the ground up strictly for commercial use, and it possessed certain elegancies unknown in other British planes of the era. Its huge fuselage, for instance, nearly as wide and as long as a railroad Pullman car and equally as comfortable contained an ornate forward cabin, a standup bar and an after cabin. Passengers enjoyed freedom of movement

INAUGURAL FLIGHT (below right). Passengers prepare to board Imperial *Argosy* for premier flight on world's first "named" route—*Silver Wing* lunch flight from Croyden to Paris, May 1, 1927, as steward (center) stands by his bar.

ARMSTRONG WHITWORTH *ARGOSY CITY OF GLASGOW* **(above left).** In center, departure time—Imperial 12-noon *Argosy II* for Europe and points East. Engines warming, baggage truck moving away, last passengers scramble aboard on port side. At right, they leave Imperial's *Argosy City of Arundel* used on London-Paris route.

throughout these compartments while in flight.

A complete catering service provided four-course hot meals to passengers on the London-Paris run—seven courses on the longer flights. Stewards served these meals on tables which separated the double seats facing each other on either side of the carpeted aisle—a convenience unknown to travelers before or since. And the location of the wings above the windows provided completely unobstructed visibility from every seat.

The passenger cabins, located forward and aft of the engines, were so thoroughly soundproofed that normal conversation could be carried on with ease. But the lavatories, cargo space and bar—relatively unimportant areas—were placed directly under and between the roaring power plants, in the noisiest part of the ship.

The four 500 HP Bristol *Jupiters,* snuggled close to each other on the leading edge of each wing to minimize yaw in the event one should fail in flight, provided such an abundance of concentrated thrust

IN FROM INDIA. Imperial Airways *Argosy II* unloads mail from Karachi. The more powerful *Jaguar IVA* engines (420 HP apiece), used on these models, extended their range and upped seating capacity to 28. Service began in 1928 using *Argosy IIs* until 1934.

that the *HP-42* could maintain altitude and operate normally on any three. This valuable characteristic provided it with a margin of safety virtually unknown in other planes of the day.

So maneuverable was this massive machine with its low 10 pound wing loading that it could be flown within the boundaries of any normal airfield with ease. It landed at a sedate 50 miles per hour and took off in nine seconds at its gross weight of 30000 pounds.

Although capable of a 136 mile-per-hour top speed, thick wings, interplane struts and huge landing gear created sufficient resistance to slow this to a more economical 105. The London-Paris flight under ideal conditions was made in two hours. But a good breeze right on the nose slowed this to a crawl and it was not unusual for the *HP-42* to take three to four hours for the 210 mile flight.

But they were amazingly economical planes and normally flew a thousand miles a day. At cruising speed they burned a mere 79 gallons an hour, or approximately 46 miles per passenger per gallon for a profit of over $150.00 per flying hour under average conditions.

SUMPTUOUS INTERIOR OF *HANNIBAL.*

SAFETY FACTOR. *DH-66 Hercules* demonstrates ability to fly with one engine out, rare feat for 1926, but important one for *DH-66* was required to fly many miles over desert areas on Cairo-Baghdad run.

HANNIBAL **CROSSES THE CHANNEL.** Lumbering and slow, giant Handley Page *Hannibals* held distinction of being first 4-engined transports to enter scheduled airline service, flying between London, Paris and Far East. Eminently safe (not a passenger fatality in years of operation) they were most comfortable planes then in existence.

95

HANNIBAL **THE RENOWNED.** First 4-engined plane built expressly for passenger carrying *H.P.-42* was probably the most famous and popular during its decade of dependable service. Most of British Royal Family and many other famous people traveled in the *Hannibals*. Below, the King (Duke of York at the time) and late Duke and Duchess of Kent are seen disembarking from *Horatius* and *Heracles* respectively at Croyden aerodrome.

Link in Britain's Far-Flung Empire

On October 30, 1936, *Canopus*—first of a fleet of 35 magnificent *S-23* Empire flying boats built by Short Brothers—entered scheduled service with Imperial Airways Ltd., in the Mediterranean.

So successful did the *S-23s* become that Imperial used them for over ten years, flying them along its Eastern and African runs, while three others, specially fitted for the task, pioneered Atlantic service in 1937. One of these, *Cavalier,* went down at sea on the Bermuda-New York run. Two others, *Caledonia* and *Cambria* completed five round trips across the Atlantic.

QANTAS also used Empire boats, for many years flying them on its Sydney-Southampton, Sydney-Durban, and Fiji Island routes—long overwater flights for which these planes proved nearly ideal.

Four *Pegasus* 9-cylinder radials of 790 HP apiece gave the *S-23* a cruising speed of 160 miles per hour. Carrying 24 passengers, their baggage, five crew members, 1½ tons of mail and 600 gallons of gasoline, cruising radius covered 800 miles, an excellent performance for the period.

The *S-23* boasted a smoking cabin in the extreme bow, containing seats for seven. Aft of this were the lavatories and a galley that served complete meals in flight. Two large cabins and a promenade area occupied the central portion of the hull, with baggage areas in the extreme rear.

As in all flying boats, passenger vision from the windows was completely unobstructed. Each seat adjusted to a number of positions, and each had its own table and reading light.

The upper deck contained the control room, occupied by pilot and copilot, navigator, radio operator and flight engineer. A storage area aft of this room carried baggage, mail and the equipment needed to convert passenger quarters for sleeping.

COORONG **IN FOR CHECKUP.** Mechanics prepare to remove prop from Number Three engine. Wheels on which massive flying boat sits are merely beaching and land-handling gear, not permanent fixture. QANTAS used *Coorong* on Sydney-Southampton run, 1938-1940 and between Sydney and Durban, 1940-1941.

QANTAS CARRIES CELEBRITY (below left). Noel Coward disembarks from QANTAS Empire Airways Ltd. (Australia) De Haviland *Rapide*. At right, passengers board British Airways Lockheed *Electra*, 1936. Over 100 of these twin-engined planes were built and delivered all over the world, proving especially valuable on short hauls and feeder line work. Powered by pair of 450 HP Pratt & Whitney *Wasp Juniors, Electras* cruised at 176 miles per hour while carrying crew of two and ten passengers.

EARLY ITALIAN TRANSPORT. This 1918 triplane designed for war use by Gianni Caproni, Italy's most prolific aeronautical engineer, was remodeled shortly after war for passenger carrying. Its double-tiered cabins (connected by staircase) contained bar, wash room and seats for 30. Pilot and co-pilot occupied open porch-like cockpit forward of upper compartment. To increase machine's performance, pair of 400 HP engines was added to original three, boosting total horse power to 2000, giving it speed of 78 miles per hour. Weighing 11,880 pounds, it carried 7700 pound payload. Wing span was 96 feet.

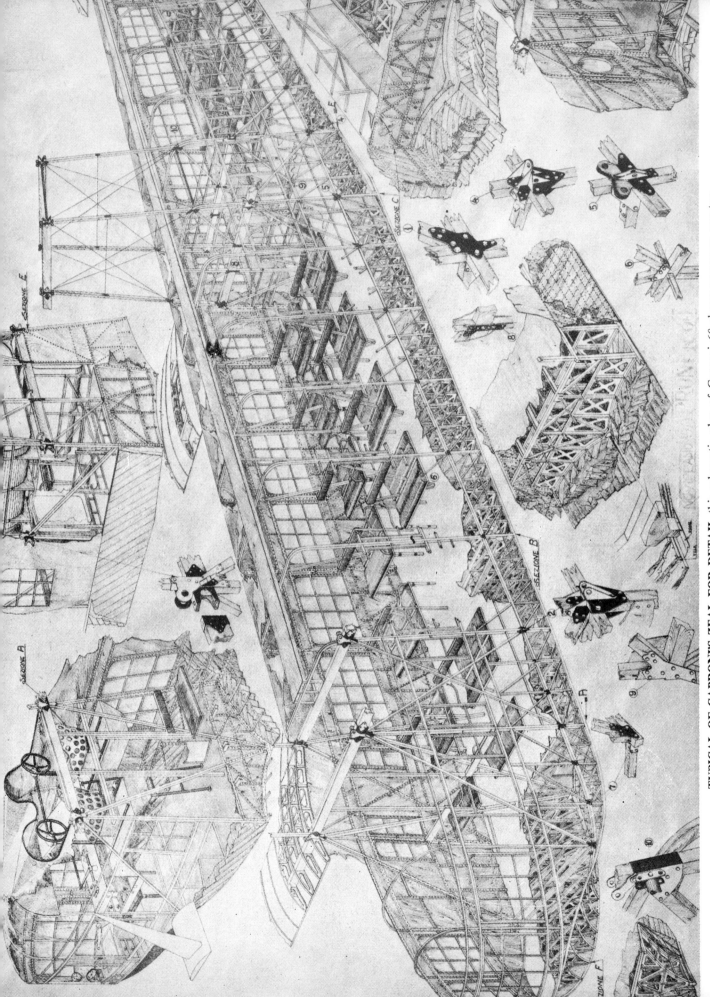

TYPICAL OF CAPRONI'S ZEAL FOR DETAIL this schematic plan of Caproni *60* shows passenger quarters and crew's compartment located above hull immediately behind and over central engine. Pilot and co-pilot sat in cockpit while other members of crew occupied enclosed cabin adjacent to it.

MODEL 60—MAGNIFICENT BID. Caproni created this nine wing monster in 1919 in attempt to provide plane capable of carrying large numbers of passengers rapidly and economically. Lack of engines powerful enough to overcome resistance of forest of struts, wires and massive frontal areas of many wings doomed ship to failure long before completion. Powered by eight 400 HP water cooled engines, big flying boat accommodated 100 passengers and weighed in excess of 30,000 pounds.

CAPRONI MODEL *60* on launching ways (above). In center, plane is shown at anchor. Lower left, three-quarter bow view—pilot cockpit located in center engine nacelle. Lower right, interior view of passenger cabin.

GREAT CAPRONI 90. Although created primarily for military use, 90 was designed for simple conversion to civil airliner for possible intercontinental use. Powered by six 1,000 HP Isotta Fraschini engines, massive machine grossed 33,000 pounds, flew at 126 miles per hour. In February 1930, it set half dozen world records for carrying capacity including one in which it lifted 22,000 pounds to 10,500 feet. This was last of massive Capronis. From this point on designer devoted his entire attention to creation of smaller, faster, more economical types.

ARTIST'S CONCEPTION OF THINGS TO COME. This 1919 drawing appeared on cover of "Scientific American" and proved amazingly accurate. Within ten years passengers would travel almost as depicted.

France Meets Challenge of the Air

By early 1921 the French had made great inroads in the passenger carrying field, thanks to Government subsidies, with no less than ten airlines linking Europe's major cities. Paris was connected to London, Brussels, Prague, Geneva, Bordeaux, Madrid and Lisbon. Other lines flew between Toulouse-Bordeaux; Toulouse-Montpelier-Marseille-Nice, and as far as Casablanca and Constantinople.

As with the British, the French used converted World War I light and heavy bombing planes modified for passenger carrying. There were Nieuports and Breguets, Salmsons and Potez *S.E.A.s* and on the Mediterranean routes, Lioré cabin flying boats. But the most famous French transports of the period were the Bleriot *Mammoths* and the Farman *Goliaths*.

The *Goliath* had been one of France's great bombers. Now, its bomb bays converted into passenger quarters, it became one of the most popular and successful transports of the day.

The pilot's cockpit, located in the center of the fuselage under the big top wing, divided the cabin into two parts. The after compartment seated eight. The forward section held six and was by far and large the most desirable part of the plane in which to ride for there was nothing to obstruct the forward vision of its occupants. It was like riding in the bombardier's "greenhouse" of a modern bomber.

The *Goliath* was a biplane powered by a pair of 260 HP air cooled Salmson radial engines. Its wing spread was 91 feet and it weighed 9,000 pounds. Its cruising speed was 72 miles per hour.

The other famous transport, the *Mammoth* was well named, for its wings spanned 110 feet and it weighed 16,000 pounds. It carried 26 passengers in elegantly upholstered settees running the length of the cabin on each side, and was powered by four 300 HP Hispano Suiza water cooled engines.

FARMAN *GOLIATH* TAKES ON PASSENGERS—1923.

THE BREGUET *14-A2 AVION SALON*

One of France's great light bombers of World War I was the Breguet *14-A2,* a medium size biplane so well designed and built that many remained in service with the French Armee de l'Air as late as 1930.

A number of these rugged machines were converted to passenger carrying, right after hostilities ended, by Companie des Messageries Aeriennes, beginning a tri-weekly trans-Channel service in 1919 later expanded to Brussels and Casablanca.

The conversion consisted of moving the pilot's seat back to the observer's, removing the tanks and installing a cabin for four in their place. The occupants appear to have had an excellent view, for the raised cabin top formed a sort of conning tower with windows on either side and dead ahead.

Substituting for the fuselage tanks was a pair of 50 gallon streamlined containers slung up under the upper wing—a throwback to pre-World War I planes which almost invariably carried their gasoline containers in this manner.

A 310 HP 12 cylinder water-cooled Renault provided the power, giving it a top speed of 118 miles per hour and a climb to 16,400 feet in 22 minutes. The ship was built entirely of aluminum except for the ribs, the trim pieces and fabric covering, a type of construction pioneered by Breguet—a factor that undoubtedly contributed to the machine's long life.

THE FARMAN *180—OISEAU BLEU*

Passenger comfort reached an all time high for the Nineteen Twenties with the lush *Oiseau Bleu,* a direct descendant of the famous wartime Farman *Goliath* bomber.

The interior of this massive biplane reflected the trend of the period toward elaborate interiors for passenger appeal. Such items as wall vases, fancy drapes and heavy carpets did nothing to improve flying ability, but they served the highly important purpose of soothing jittery travelers with their home-like appearance. And they impressed the neophyte by the mere fact that the plane was big and powerful enough to carry such ornate and useless devices.

The *Oiseau Bleu* went one better; it carried a bar, a genuine mahogany one with a brass rail extending around its top to which customers could cling during bumpy weather. This little luxury item stood amidship on the port side and was attended by a steward who served food as well as drinks.

Indirect lighting, double thick sound-proofed walls, overhead baggage racks, reclining over-stuffed chairs, big windows and standing headroom plus the privilege of moving about the cabin while in flight all contributed to a feeling of well being for its passengers.

This plane was used exclusively by "Lignes Aeriennes Farman" and began service in 1929 on the Paris-Brussels - Antwerp - Rotterdam - Amsterdam - Berlin runs. At one point during its development Farman entertained the wild idea of using it to fly the Atlantic, but nothing came of it.

The outstanding design characteristic of this handsome biplane was the tandem arrangement of its engines. These 500 HP, 12 cylinder Hispano Suizas, located high above the fuselage (thereby contributing in a large degree to cabin quietness) placed the center of thrust of their 4 blade propellers directly on the center of the upper wing. Not only did this disposition of the power plants direct prop wash over the top of the wing, where it would do the most good, but it completely eliminated yaw during single engine operation.

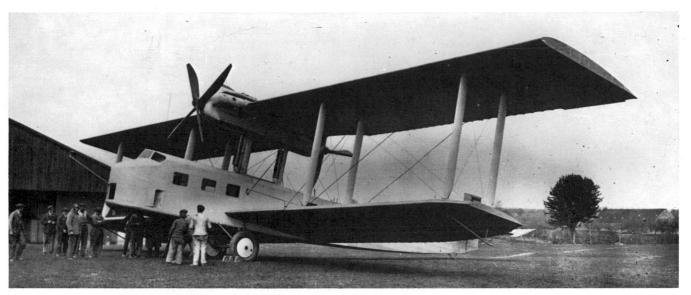

BLUE BIRD OVER FRANCE (above). *Oiseau Bleu,* Farman 180, attracted passengers by its elaborate furnishings, stand up bar, roomy cabin. Used exclusively by Lignes Ariennes Farman, it began service in 1929, at one point casting covetous eyes on Atlantic run.

CONVERTED LIGHT BOMBER (below). This Breguet *14-A2* served France well in World War I after which it was used in passenger carrying by Companie des Messageries Aeriennes on tri-weekly Channel crossings and later between Brussels and Casablanca.

BUFFOONERY AT LE BOURGET (below). Characters in this publicity act photo are fake, but Lufthansa's Focke-Wolf *A-17a* and surroundings at Le Bourget are genuine.

PRE-FLIGHT CONFERENCE (above). Direct air service from Le Bourget to Berlin in eight hours began May 26, 1926 with this Farman *F-170* highwing monoplane. Powered by 500 HP Farman engine, *F-170* cruised at slightly over 100 miles per hour with eight passengers and baggage. Pilot sat in enclosed cockpit high up near wing's leading edge directly behind engine, with cargo and baggage stowed in compartment beneath.

CRACK UP! (below left). Farman *Goliath* on Brussels-Paris run hit soft earth on takeoff. Right—appointments worthy of a king. Known as richest-looking passenger carrier in service, French Caudron *C-81's* cabin reflected trend of times for lavish fittings and furnishings. Compagnie Franco-Roumaine de Navigation Aerriene flew this ship extensively in 1924.

Compania Mexicana de Aviacion

Mexican commercial aviation can attribute its birth to roaming bands of highway robbers. In the "Klondike days" of the Mexican oil fields centering around Tampico on the Republic's northeast side, paymasters travelling to the isolated oil camps were constantly waylaid and robbed by highjackers who stalked them along jungle trails.

As time went on, the job of paymaster became increasingly more dangerous. The loss to the oil companies assumed serious proportions but there seemed to be no solution to the problem. And then one day a Tampico banker hit on the idea of delivering the money by air, thereby marking him as a man of great imagination and forethought, for Mexico in 1924 was anything but an air minded country.

Fortunately for everyone concerned except the outlaws, a band of roving pilots, barnstorming through Mexico in search of a fast buck landed at Tampico about this time, and quickly sold their four Lincoln Standard biplanes to the Tampico banker who obviously knew a good thing when he saw it. Thus, in the office of a Tampico Notary Public, on August 20, 1924 was born Compania Mexicana de Aviacion—today's oldest Latin American airline—with a pasture-landing field a few kilometers from Tampico, and a flight of 93 miles across jungle wastes to the booming oil fields in Tuxpan.

The airplane has always been a tremendous success in countries with nearly inaccessible areas, and Mexico was no exception. In no time, CMA had increased its scope spreading out to other cities: Veracruz, Tejeria, Mexico City, soon abandoning the single passenger Standards in favor of 6-place Fairchild cabin monoplanes, far faster and more profitable to operate.

PAYMASTER TOOK TO THE AIR in one of these 2-place 150 HP *Lincoln Standards* when Compania Mexicana de Aviacion was formed in 1924 to outwit payroll bandits.

CHECKERED FLAG GAVE ALL-CLEAR for want of control and radio tower in 1928. Plane shown is 6-place Fairchild *71* cabin monoplane owned by Compania Mexicana de Aviacion. Center—airport jitney. CMA transported its Vera Cruz-bound passengers in this rail car to airport in Tejeria during mid-Twenties—one of first world efforts to provide ground passage to and from airports. Right, 2-place *Lincoln Standard* used on CMA's jungle run, carrying lone passenger across mountains and jungles between Tampico and Tuxpan oil fields in 1924.

QANTAS of Australia

Scheduled flight operation in Australia began shortly after the end of World War I when QANTAS, now one of the world's largest airlines, introduced a service between Charleville and Cloncurry—300 miles across Queensland bush, punctuated by a halfway refuelling stop at Longreach.

Flying equipment consisted of one war-surplus Armstrong Whitworth *FK-8* a two place observation machine, a type that had given a good account of itself during the latter days of the War. Its 160 HP water cooled Beardmore engine gave it a maximum speed of 95 miles per hour and a cruising speed of 84. Barring headwinds and including time out at Longreach, a passenger could count on making the trip in just short of five hours.

Early in 1923 QANTAS acquired a *DH-9C* converted to carry three passengers in what was probably the oddest arrangement ever devised for this old workhorse. One occupant sat in an open cockpit directly behind the pilot, while the other two perched in a third cockpit in back, one facing forward and one aft. A hinged metal cover semi-enclosed it, affording protection from the sun and rain to its occupants while providing vision for them through an eight inch gap on either side.

A more satisfactory layout for passenger comfort, however, was the *DH-50a,* six of which QANTAS introduced in 1924. Largely developed out of the experience of Aeroplane Hire Service of London, it proved to be Australia's most successful post-war transport.

KLM—Royal Dutch Airlines

Dutch enthusiasm in aviation reached an almost fever pitch in the fall of 1919 when more than 500,000 persons attended a six week "aviation meeting" in Amsterdam. Designed to promote interest in commercial flying, the meet was a huge success, 4,000 daring persons paying 40 guilders apiece for sightseeing trips in war surplus *DH-9s* converted for passenger hopping by the simple expedient of removing the double-yolked machine gun from the rear cockpit.

As a result of the meet, aviation became a topic of conversation throughout the entire country, and plans for a Dutch air transport company assumed definite shape. By Oct. 7, 1919 the "Koninklijke Luchtvaart Maatschappij" more conveniently called KLM, or Royal Dutch Airlines, was founded in The Hague.

In these formative days, with little or no experience in operating air services, the company wisely entered into a charter agreement with the British

WAR VETERAN (below). Ancient British *BE2E* observation machine built in 1916 was still in use in Queensland and Northern Territory Aerial Service (QANTAS) in Australia for taxi work and joy rides in 1921. Bottom—first cabin plane in Australia. For the first time in Australian history, with this De Haviland *DH-50,* a passenger could fly without helmet and goggles.

ACROSS THE QUEENSLAND BUSH QANTAS *DH9C* loads passengers and baggage at Longreach.

FOKKER *F-2* **MONOPLANE** carried passengers in unprecedented comfort.

carrier, Air Transport & Travel Ltd., by then relatively well established in the business. On May 17, 1920, using one of AT&T Ltd's. *DH-16s,* KLM inaugurated a trial flight between Amsterdam and London, and thence operated on alternate days. This, the earliest connection in the world to be flown by a carrier still in operation today gives KLM the distinction of being the oldest airline in continuous service in the World.

The *DH-9s* and *16s* used on these early runs carried no radios, and their instruments (a generally unreliable compass, an airspeed indicator, tachometer, oil pressure gauge and fuel gauge) were hardly adequate for long over-water flights. As a result, pilots shunned them as much as possible. KLM's Amsterdam-London planes took a U-shaped course flying south to the narrowest part of the Channel between Calais and Folkstone and thence north to London. Blackboards laid out along the route informed the pilot of weather conditions ahead. If the messages indicated rain or fog or strong winds, the pilot turned back.

In September of that year, with aircraft leased from a German line, KLM opened a second service —Amsterdam to Bremen, Hamburg and Copenhagen.

Much of KLM's flying during these embryonic months of 1920 had been done in open cockpit planes, a state of affairs that demanded a high degree of sportsmanship from the passengers, who, with little or no other choice open to them, gratefully accepted the leather coats and helmets, the gloves and goggles and an occasional hot water bottle, all provided by the line at no extra expense.

But by the spring of 1921, KLM had its own planes—Fokker *11s,* 185 HP cabin monoplanes carrying five passengers in unprecedented comfort, only the pilot remaining out in the open.

That same year the line introduced the *F-111,* a larger, faster version of the *F-11,* powered by a 230 HP water-cooled Siddley *Puma* engine which shared the pilot's cockpit, with nothing separating airman and roaring machinery but a thin metal bulkhead. A tremendously stable machine with a low landing speed, it proved ideal for the small air fields of the day. Its cabin contained an upholstered bench for three, two comfortable chairs, a heater, vases, curtains, and space for luggage. This was traveling in style for 1921.

KLM was on its way. In May it opened one of the world's first air ticket offices; it introduced a bus service from metropolitan areas to the airports; it built a hotel-restaurant for the convenience of aerial travelers at Schiphol Airport. By 1925 it had become the first airline to use air cooled engines and all metal propellers, two factors that produced greater economy and reliability.

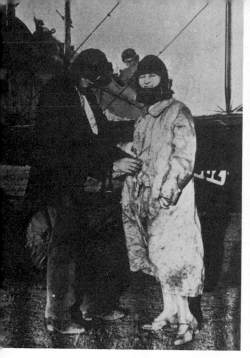

BUSH FLYING DOWN UNDER (above left). It was muddy and cold that day at one of outback Queensland's airstrips. QANTAS pilot adjusts warm overcoat on woman passenger before making flight in Armstrong-Whitworth *FK-8*. Center, KLM Fokker *F-3* takes on passengers, 1921. Right, KLM's first cabin plane in 1921—Fokker *F-2* monoplane.

GUESTS DROP IN FOR THE NIGHT. Two women passengers arrive at "Old Barn" in Hildenborough, Australia, said to be the world's first cafe to have its own landing field. No date is given for event but judging by plane—a World War I Avro *504K* trainer—it must have been around 1919.

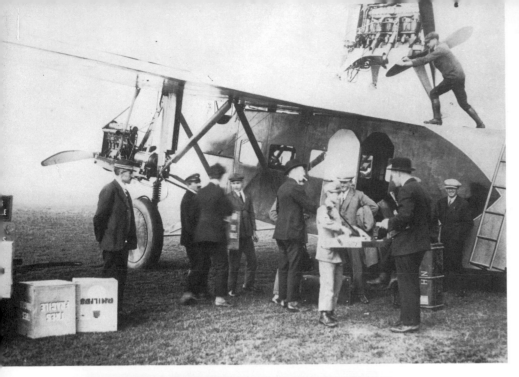

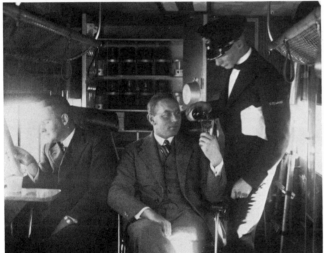

EXTRA ENGINE FOR GOOD MEASURE (above left). Passengers prepare to board KLM Dutch Koolhaven aircraft used on Amsterdam-Paris run. This peculiar machine with two un-cowled wing engines, third one atop the cabin, carried eight. Pilot sat forward in open cockpit. It is assumed top engine created high decibal count in passenger quarters and must have been a killer to start.

SUPER SPECIAL FOKKER *7* **(above center).** KLM operated world's first intercontinental charter flight (Amsterdam to Java and back) for an American newspaper owner. Time—35 days.

ALL THIS AND HEAVEN TOO? (left). Luxury service aboard KLM Fokker *10* tri-motor in 1930. Open door discloses steward's silverware and glass supply. (Below left) Fokker *F-7* in flight.

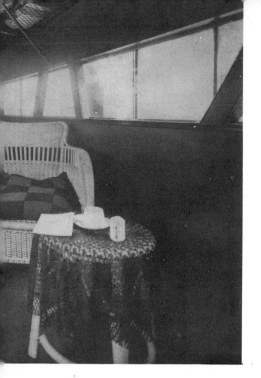

ONE WAY TO FUEL (above right). Lack of suitable facilities in 1927 made this crude method of gassing up necessary. *Fokker F-7* carried spare wheel along with cans of gasoline. (Right) Interior of standard *F-7*.

ROTTERDAM SHOPPER'S SPECIAL (below center). Housewives from the Dutch province of Zeeland radiate happiness in anticipation of takeoff in a Fokker *8* on a KLM domestic run.

TWIN-ENGINED 12-PASSENGER FOKKER *8* — 1927 (below right) predecessor of famous Fokker tri-motor used on KLM's European network. While helmeted pilot and copilot attend to last minute details beside the plane, mechanics check out engines oblivious to fact passengers are climbing aboard.

German Flying Goes Commercial

The groundwork for a commercial airline in post-war Germany was laid with extraordinary foresight in 1917 by Deutsche Luft-Reederei (German Air Navigation Co.), a corporation organized for the express purpose of investigating the feasibility of such a venture.

By February 1919, Luft-Reederei succeeded in opening and maintaining an air service between Berlin and Weimar, using World War I machines primitively converted for passenger carrying. These planes were far from satisfactory, no more suited to the job than the converted military planes used at the time in other nations. But aerial transportation was a new business, and no such thing as an out-and-out passenger plane existed anywhere in the world. Furthermore, people itched to fly after four years of hearing about airplanes and watching their fantastically rapid development. It was war-surplus equipment or nothing. Other lines sprang up throughout the country encouraged by Luft-Reederei's success and eventually all were consolidated into Deutsche Luft-Hansa—Germany's one great Government-subsidized airline. The demand for better planes became acute.

RUMBLE SEAT FOR TWO. Housing over aft cockpit represented step toward modern passenger comfort when this Fokker *D-VII* (Germany's most potent World War I fighter) was modified into commercial type. Note door in side and stirrup installed for convenience in entering. Transformation consisted of lengthening fuselage and enclosing aft cockpit. Powered by 220 HP Mercedes, war time version flew at 135 miles per hour wide open.

BUILT TO BOMB LONDON. German 5-engined Staaken *Giant* bomber hastily converted into 25 passenger transport immediately after World War I. 75 mile per hour machine, with wing spread of 134 feet, was powered by pair of 245 HP Maybachs in each wing nacelle and single Maybach in nose. Little is known of this plane's history as passenger carrier but it must have been short, planes of this type considered inefficient in all respects.

Junkers F-13—First All-Metal Low Wing

The Versailles Treaty, which prohibited Germany from building military aircraft, proved a blessing of sorts to commercial lines, for aircraft manufacturers were forced into commercial plane construction. In the ensuing years, it created some of the finest transports the world had ever seen.

One of the first machines designed especially for airline use in Germany was the *Junkers*—a low wing monoplane far ahead of its time when it appeared late in 1919. This machine, epitomized in the Model *F-13,* was internally braced—a distinct innovation in 1919—and powered by a Junkers 185 HP water cooled engine, cruised at 106 miles per hour. It carried four passengers in its cabin, seated in comfortable armchairs, while a fifth rode in the open

pilot's cockpit forward of the wing. Fully loaded, it weighed 4070 pounds, 1540 pounds of which were payload.

Its corrugated metal skin-covering distinguished it from all other planes of the day, and the absence of struts and braces gave it what then must have been an honest-to-goodness "new look."

This was the world's first successful metal low wing, so successful in fact that its basic design has been copied and recopied down to the present day.

A long series of Junkers all-metal transports followed the *F-13* (one of which was still used by Lufthansa as late as 1931) until production shifted entirely to the reborn manufacture of bombers—for use in World War II.

FIRST ALL-METAL LOW WING PLANE (above left)—
the Junkers *F-13,* internally braced and powered by
Junkers 185 HP water-cooled engine. Advanced design has
been employed in many later airplanes.

LUFT HANSA WORKHORSE (above right). Junkers'
first tri-motor, *G-24,* provided comfortable accommodations for
ten passengers while pilot and copilot sat forward in open
cockpit. This was world's first low wing tri-motor and flew
extensively on Luft Hansa's long European routes. Fitted
with three Junkers air-cooled radials of 280 to 310 HP
each, the *24* cruised at 100 miles per hour. Below center,
interior of *G-24.*

FAMOUS GERMAN TRANSPORT (below left). Focke-
Wolf *A-17a* monoplane powered by single 480 HP Siemens
Jupiter 9-cyc. air cooled radial engine. Extensively used by
Luft-Hansa and number of small feeder lines because of
exceptional stability in air (a distinct passenger appeal)
A-17s did yeoman duty over distances ranging from 450
to 750 miles. This was a high wing, internally-braced monoplane, comfortably seating eight passengers and equipped
with dual controls for pilot and copilot. Huge for a single
engined plane, it weighed nearly 9,000 pounds loaded and
spanned 65 feet. Note size of landing wheels and 4-blade
propeller.

DINNER IS SERVED (below center) on the Berlin-Vienna
air express—a deluxe arrangement of *Junkers-31* tri-motor
carrying 12 first class passengers—1928. The "high density"
version of this fast monoplane contained aisle seats attached
to right hand row thereby upping capacity to 17. Large
bunker beneath cabin floor contained baggage while cargo
was carried in special compartment between cockpit and
cabin, an area shared by wireless operator. Lavatories were
located in rear of cabin.

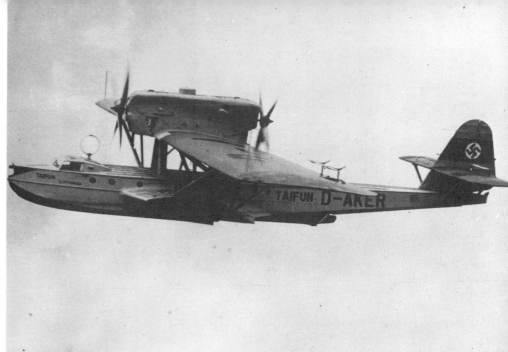

LUFT HANSA DORNIER WAL FLYING BOAT (above right). Introduced in Germany in 1922 these high-performance seaplanes were used for long range over-water transportation of mail and passengers through the Twenties and Thirties. *Wal* was characterized by high parasol wing and clump of either two or four engines mounted atop center section.

ALL ASHORE THAT'S GOING ASHORE (right). One difficulty in carrying passengers by seaplane is clearly demonstrated here as Dornier *Wal* discharges group into waiting launch. No other method of loading and unloading was possible if there were no suitable docking facilities or they could not be used because of weather conditions.

Twenty Years Too Soon

In early 1929 Germany launched what was then the largest airplane ever built. Weighing an unheard of 52 tons, the Giant *DO-X* could carry 100 persons with ease (it once carried 152) and was designed expressly for trans-Atlantic service.

Measuring 157 feet from wing tip to wing tip (a *DC-7C* spans 127 feet) and 137 feet from bow to stern, it towered an impressive 28 feet above the surface. Three decks inside its huge hull housed the cargo holds and tanks, the passenger compartments, and the bridge. The latter contained the pilot and co-pilot seats, radio room, navigators' compartment and an engine control station—probably the first ever carried on an airplane.

A minimum of 6000 HP—far more than even Germany's war time Zeppelins had carried aloft—was needed to get this colossus airborne. Twelve of the most powerful engines of the day—500 HP Siemens *Jupiter* air cooled radials—were mounted above the wing on inter-connecting nacelles, six pushing and six pulling.

The frontal resistance of a 9-cylinder air cooled engine imposes a serious drag on any aircraft, and a large portion of the Dornier's 6000 horses was

DO-X **TAXIS SLOWLY** as members of her crew stand by on forward deck to handle its docking lines.

consumed in pulling 12 of them through the air. Streamlined cowlings had not been invented, but it is doubtful if they would have helped, for even in their uncovered state the rear bank overheated badly. Further serious drag was induced by the massive structure on which the power plants were mounted, but because this allowed access to them during flight, some sacrifice in efficiency was considered justified.

A passageway in the wing leading to each of the six engine nacelles allowed the crew of eight engineers to make repairs while in the air. Before a flight it was customary to place two of the engineers in the control room to man the switches and throttles while the other six started the engines from the nacelles. Immediately before takeoff, the two inboard engineers joined the engine room force to help in the intricate procedure of getting the huge ship airborne, while the four men in the outboard nacelles remained in them during flight.

The pilot's sole control of the engines was through two throttles, one for each side of the plane. A panel of 12 lights mounted before him indicated which were running and which were off.

The tremendous thrust developed by this great battery of engines gave the *DO-X* amazing performance—when lightly loaded. With 60 people aboard, no cargo and very little fuel, its takeoff time averaged 33 seconds. With four engines out, it once took to the air in 28 seconds with 25 aboard, no cargo, and only partly full tanks. With 100 people and an all-up weight of 108,000 pounds it became airborne after a 60 second run and flew six hours—its maximum endurance—at 111 miles per hour.

But the *DO-X* was too far ahead of its time and the lack of high powered engines spoiled its chances of ever becoming a profitable transport. In an effort to reduce drag of the air cooled *Jupiters*, 600 HP Curtiss *Conquerors* were substituted late in 1930. But the added 1200 HP derived from these heavier American engines did little to improve the overall performance, and its trip from Germany to the United States was anything but a spectacular success.

Leaving Friedrichshafen in November, 1930, it arrived in New York harbor on August 27, 1931. Dogged by bad weather, an almost catastrophic fire, head winds and engine trouble, it soon became the laughing stock of the aeronautical world.

In America, a number of successful passenger carrying flights were made, but any hope its designers held that United States airlines might be interested in using the 12-engined plane had long since vanished.

In a final effort to impress the world with the feasibility of trans-Atlantic travel by heavier-than-air machines, the *DO-X* left New York for a nonstop return flight to Europe. Loaded to the hilt with fuel, it barely staggered off the water, and for the first eight hours failed to gain over 50 feet of altitude. Under such conditions, failure of a single engine would have brought the massive machine back to the surface.

And so ended a bold and brilliant attempt to begin aerial transportation on a grand scale—an attempt unfortunately made 20 years too soon.

FRONTAL DRAG. Lack of streamlining on the massive hull of *DO-X* accounts in part for its inability to fly efficiently.

FIFTY-TWO TONS AHEAD OF THEIR TIME, Giant Dornier *DO-X* built for trans-Atlantic service carried 100 persons with ease. 12 engines delivered 6000 HP but not enough for profitable operation.

CABIN OF *DO-X.* Although obviously a publicity shot, view shows elegance of passenger quarters. Use of movable armchairs, opening portlights, heavy curtains, wall-to-wall carpeting and fancy wallpaper indicates effort made by Dornier to provide maximum passenger comfort and home-like atmosphere.

PIONEER COLONIAL AIRLINER. 300 HP Levy *Lepen* 3-place seaplane flew 350 miles regularly between Leopoldville and Stanleyville in Belgian Congo in 1920 for SNETA, predecessor of SABENA, probably first colonial airline in world.

SHORT HAUL WONDER De Haviland *Rapide*, famous for operating profitably on less than full load in day when capacity loading was exception. *Rapides* continued in active service on British and Empire airways long after World War II with many still operating today. Plane shown here remains in constant use with British European Airways on 20 minute flight between Lands End and the Scillies. Cruising at 117 miles per hour *Rapide* can carry seven passengers and baggage.

America Comes From Behind

For three years following the birth of flight, the Wrights flew their machines in ever widening circles —longer and higher and further than the preceding ones—while elsewhere in the world not a soul succeeded in getting off the ground for even an instant.

But in spite of this amazing contribution to aviation, once the secret leaked out to other countries America lagged far behind in its development. Like a retarded child with a toy it cannot seem to understand or use, it stood idly by as others enjoyed it to the hilt. For whereas in America a mere handful of enthusiasts existed, in Europe the art of flying mushroomed into a major attraction.

There were moments of triumph for Americans, of course: Glenn Curtiss' smashing victory in the Gordon Bennet race at Rheims, 1909; Johnstone's altitude record of 9714 feet at the Belmont meet in 1910; the winning of the Gordon Bennett race in 1911 by Weymann—on a French machine. But these were small achievements for a nation that had invented the flying machine. All the truly great accomplishments, the speed and distance, the altitude and weight-carrying records of the world belonged to France and England and Germany where records fell nearly as fast as they were made.

America showed her shamefully backward position when World War 1 caught her flat footed. Not a plane in the country could meet the exacting requirements of aerial warefare. As a matter of fact, the United States had produced less than 200 planes *all told* between the Wrights' 1903 flight and 1917. (By way of comparison Germany had entered the war three years before with better than 250 first line aircraft.) By 1918, however, America had produced better than 2500 aircraft although no more than a few dozen saw any front line service.

There followed further stagnation in the American aviation industry as hostilities ended in Europe. What flying existed at that point consisted of curtailed military operations and unorganized barnstorming by ex-military pilots. These gypsy flyers, still enthralled by flying, many of them knowing no other profession, were the true pioneers of aerial transport in the United States. To every man, woman and child who would venture to their cowpasture airports throughout the country, they preached the gospel of flying, enticing them into their flimsy planes— their surplus Army *Jennys* and *Standards* and *DH-4s*.

For the most part these machines were completely unsuited for the type of work required of them— stunting and passenger carrying—but there was no choice. Nothing else existed and no manufacturer considered the market lucrative enough to introduce anything better.

Mainstay of the barnstormer's business was the joy hop—a three minute ride costing anywhere from five to fifteen bucks depending on how sporty the crowd happened to be. Thousands of Americans learned about flying on one of these rides in the open cockpit behind the roaring *OX-5s* and *Hispano-Suizas*. This was the thrill supreme, to lean out past the windshield and smell the oily warmth of the engine in the slipstream rushing past, to feel the gale tearing at cheeks and hair and lips, and the tears streaming out of half-closed eyes.

Out of this casual operation gradually grew sense, however. The fixed base operator appeared—the pilot with a plane and maybe more than one plane— and perhaps an old barn which he called a hangar, on which he tacked a wind sock. He specialized in student instruction, joy hopping and taxi work—the first step toward carrying people from one point to another by air.

Nowhere in America did flying meet with the enthusiastic response which greeted it in Europe, however. Shorter distances between European cities (ideal for ex-War planes with limited cruising radiuses) plus Government subsidizing, gave foreign aviation a boost unhappily lacking in America. A few daring operators made scattered attempts throughout the country at flying passengers on scheduled flights in the early Nineteen Twenties, but ignored by an apathetic government and public, their operations withered and died.

The picture was not entirely black, however, for the nation led the world in mail and express carrying, beginning a scheduled service on May 15, 1918 which expanded under the impetus of Government contracts to a point where in 1923 it linked New York and San Francisco. Trips increased with astounding rapidity from 793 in 1918 to 4071 in 1924, and interspersed with the mail bags could often be found an occasional passenger, obligingly carried by an operator with an eye to the future.

Commercial aviation fell under the regulations of the Federal Government in 1926 with the passage of the Air Commerce Act. The bill culminated 14 years of discussions and arguments for Government control, and with its birth began the development of civil aeronautics in the United States.

Previous to the act's passage, a haphazard system of inspection and operations existed throughout the country. Some operators and individuals were naturally more cautious than others, but in no case did a code of ethics or a system of maintenance exist, and aircraft passengers put their lives squarely in the hands of their unlicensed pilots, and their trust in whatever individual systems of plane and engine upkeep the owners cared to use.

The new act changed all this and started commercial and private aviation along a straight and narrow path. Basically, the Act provided for the establishment of civil airways with lights, emergency fields, beacons and other aids; the inspection and licensing of aircraft new and old; the establishment of rules and regulations governing construction of aircraft; the licensing of pilots; the charting of airways and the publication of maps; the promotion of aerial transportation—all vitally needed to stimulate commercial aviation and to make flying safe.

And stimulate it, it did. Whereas in 1926 there had been but 19 operators in the country, the majority of them individuals, by 1927 there were 24 who flew a total of 5,242,839 miles while 27 operators the following year flew 10,470,000. That year 12,594 passengers were carried on scheduled lines; in 1928 the number had jumped to 52,934.

The Act took the guesswork out of aircraft operation and upkeep and laid down ground rules for the entire industry. Transport aviation settled down and tended to the business of providing safe and dependable travel by air.

AMERICA'S FIRST CABIN PLANE? American-built, Liberty-powered *DH-4* used in U.S. for passenger carrying postal employees in 1919. Conversion differed from most in that pilot's cockpit was moved back into observer's and passengers tucked into enclosed cubbyhole immediately behind engine.

First Foreign Flight Service—New York to Havana

Early in 1920, Aeromarine Airways Corp. inaugurated a regular service between Key West, Florida and Havana, thereby becoming the first scheduled airline to fly between the U. S. and a foreign country.

Converted Navy *HS-2* coastal patrol seaplanes, powered by single 330 HP *Liberty* engines, were used on this run, carrying four passengers in two open cockpits. Thanks to Government mail subsidies, this operation succeeded from the start, and the following year Aeromarine began hauling passengers all the way from New York.

Two days were required for this flight with stops at Atlantic City, Beaufort, South Carolina, Miami and Key West—a quick flight for the majority of passengers, whose business in Havana centered mainly around its bars. For these were prohibition days and the American thirst had become acute.

On this run Aeromarine used converted Navy *F-5-L* flying boats, larger than the *HS-2s,* and equipped with two luxurious passenger cabins seating fourteen—six in the forward compartment, eight in the aft. Large round portlights provided reasonably unobstructed views for the occupants.

Aeromarine went all out on an advertising campaign designed to stir up interest in its aerial routes, and it succeeded, to a certain point. By the year's end it owned six *F-5-Ls* and six *HS-2s,* and its service had been expanded to cover Albany, Montreal and Chicago. Over 6000 passengers were carried on these routes without injuring a soul.

In June 1922 it added a Cleveland-Detroit service, making two round trips a day. The flight took 90 minutes, a fact proclaimed by the slogan "The Ninety Minute Line" painted on the *F-5-Ls'* hulls in large white letters.

But the public remained indifferent to this modern means of transportation. Too many people feared flying and no amount of persuasion could get them off the ground. This made tough sledding for pioneer airline operators and Aeromarine was no exception. In spite of a letter-perfect safety record and an excellent schedule efficiency, not enough people could be enticed into aerial travel to make it a paying proposition, and after a brave struggle to keep its head above water, Aeromarine went out of business in 1923. Many years would lapse before the routes it pioneered would be flown again.

California Takes to the Air

Early in the Nineteen Twenties, T. Claude Ryan, the young manager of a small but flourishing flying service in California, expanded his flying equipment from a single *JN4-D Jenny* to a fleet of six World War 1 surplus Standard biplane trainers. Originally 2-place open cockpit machines, Ryan converted them into 5-place cabin "transports" and used them at first for sightseeing trips around the San Diego area.

Rebuilt and repowered by new 150 HP Hispano Suiza engines, these Ryan-Standards entered service on the Los Angeles-San Diego run on March 1, 1925, a regularly-scheduled, year around passenger airline created and operated by Ryan.

The line flew one round trip a day with a flying time of 1½ hours each way. The fare was $17.50 one way; $26.50 for the round trip. With one passenger a day each way, Ryan figured the venture would break even. (Today's flight time for the trip is under three quarters of an hour and the round trip is about $17.00.)

Ryan's advertising extolled the wonders of traveling by air. "From the beginning of time, advancement in civilization has been marked by improvement in methods of transportation" a Ryan Airlines folder gushed. "The inauguration of Airway Service reveals the most perfect form of travel known to man."

The literature assured prospective passengers that the "Company's rigid system of plane inspection and maintenance, the employment of only the best pilots and mechanics, is ample assurance of safe and delightful trips."

Enthusiastic over the prospects of air transportation, Ryan later in 1925 acquired the first plane built by Donald Douglas, the *Cloudster,* forerunner of the world-famous series of Douglas transports. The *Cloudster* was built in 1920, and possessed the distinction of being the first airplane to carry successfully the equivalent of its own weight.

Again a remodelling job was necessary, and the *Cloudster* was changed from its original configuration of three open cockpits for eight, into a single cabin seating eleven. A door in the forward part of the cabin opened into the pilot and co-pilot's cockpit which remained exposed to the elements, protected only by a windshield.

Occupants of this big single-engined biplane enjoyed the luxury of moving about to a limited degree in the cabin, a pleasure very much denied the Ryan-Standard passengers who were forced to sit tight in their noisy, claustrophobia-provoking little cuddies.

Ryan piled up an impressive record of carrying 5616 passengers in 1926, while flying a total of 75,690 miles.

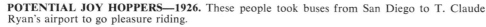

POTENTIAL JOY HOPPERS—1926. These people took buses from San Diego to T. Claude Ryan's airport to go pleasure riding.

PASSENGER PAMPERING IN 1919 (above left). An attempt to supply some sort of passenger comfort was provided by Aeromarine Plane and Motor Company in its Model *50C* flying boat by enclosing the 2-place cockpit with transparent hood. This 3-place seaplane, powered by 130 HP Aeromarine *Type L* engine, was designed primarily for charter work and aerial commuting. With half ton of machinery above and behind them occupants of such pusher planes rode in imminent danger of being crushed in event of crash. But for ease of docking on water the pusher seaplane could not be surpassed and with exhaust and propeller far behind, noise level in cockpits was reduced to minimum.

LINKING HAVANA TO DRY U.S. (above center). With prohibition taking its toll in this country Aeromarine Airways used converted Navy *F-5-L* flying boats to inaugurate two-day service from New York and East Coast cities to Havana.

WICKER CHAIR ERA (left). Forward cabin of 14 passenger *F-5-L* flying boat *Santa Maria* used by Aeromarine Airways Inc. on its New York-Havana run. This compartment seated six. After one—behind the pilot's open cockpits—accommodated eight. Door in front end led to forward cockpit used during docking operations and for loading and unloading passengers. Note round portlights, each with roll up shade, and skylight.

TOP BRASS INAUGURATES NEW AIR LINE (top right).
Henry Ford, Edsel Ford and William Mayo come out to bid
pilot Eddie Hamilton bon voyage on maiden voyage of Stout
Transport, later known as Stout Air Service, 1925. At right,
Stout *2-AT* interior with bare metal walls and floor, semi-
circular windows that opened halfway, exposed structural
beams and all-metal ceiling.

TIN GOOSE PROTOTYPE (below). Stout *2-AT,* first all-
metal plane operated on U.S. airlines, preceded Ford's
famous *Tri-Motor.* Single 400 HP *Liberty* engine propelled
this monoplane at better than 100 miles per hour.

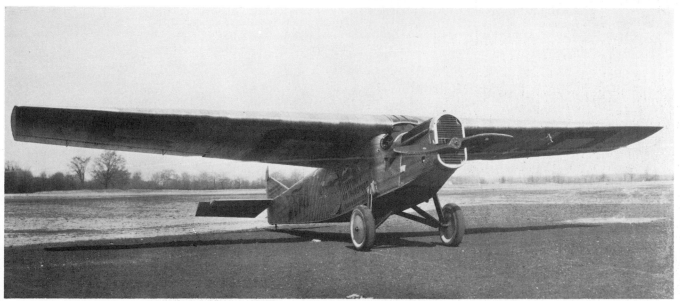

First All-Metal Commercial Plane in U.S.

One of the more remarkable planes to be used on an early American airway system was the Stout *2-AT,* the direct predecessor of the Ford *Tri-Motor,* and the first all-metal plane to be used commercially in the country.

Powered by a single 400 HP *Liberty* engine, the *Air Transport* carried eight passengers and two pilots at better than a hundred miles an hour, the relatively great power of its big war surplus engine giving it unusually good performance for the day.

Eleven *2-ATs* were built, first by the Stout Metal Plane Company, and later by its successor, the Ford Motor Company, between 1924 and late 1925. Used mainly by Ford's own freight line, Stout Air Service and Florida Airways, these planes piled up many thousands of hours on scheduled routes between 1925 and 1928.

Ford alone flew over 575,000 miles with its fleet of four *2-ATs,* one of which alone accounted for 132,000 miles or nearly 1400 hours—a phenomenal amount of time for a plane in 1925.

Stout Air Service, which began scheduled runs in September 1925 used the *2-ATs* exclusively for nearly three years on its Detroit, Chicago, Cleveland and Grand Rapids routes.

Florida Airways, founded in 1925 by World War I aces Eddie Rickenbacker and Reed Chambers using one Curtiss *Lark* and two *OXX6 Travelairs,* purchased four *2-ATs* from the Ford Motor Company in December, and immediately commenced scheduled passenger service between Miami, Ft. Myers, Tampa, Jacksonville, Atlanta and Macon. In seven months of operation it carried 939 passengers—hardly an imposing volume—but its operating efficiency averaged 90% and was unmarred by passenger fatalities.

But like so many aerial ventures of the day, losses exceeded the profits. Two of the *2-ATs* crashed, one was taken over by the creditors and by mid-1927 the company sold out to a subsidiary of Pan American Airways, which at the time had still to make its first flight.

MAIL MUST GO THROUGH! Attitude of air mail carriers toward passengers in mid-Nineteen Twenties is epitomized in this picture of one lonely fare patiently awaiting arrival of U.S. airmail bags. Passengers were carried reluctantly and only if room remained after stowing mail.

Barnstorming in Kansas

(Reprinted from "Aviation" July 14, 1924)

"One of the largest crowds ever attracted by flying exhibitions in the Middle West was assembled at the flying field at Lincoln, Nebraska on May 25 to watch the performance of the Lincoln Standard Aircraft Corp. planes assisted by five Army deHavilands from Ft. Riley, Kan. The program of the afternoon was made up of airplane races, parachute jumping and special stunt work.

A record for passenger carrying was undoubtedly made during the afternoon when three Lincoln Standard planes carried 408 people. The afternoon receipts totaled $1194.00, making a total of 398 pay passengers carried at $3.00 per head, ten guards riding during the afternoon as free passengers. Bob Cochrane of Casper, Wyo., flying a new Lincoln Standard five-place plane carried 184 people. Earl Barnes, flying another Lincoln Standard five-place plane carried 169.

At no time during the afternoon was there a lull in obtaining passengers and the popularity of the LS5 as a passenger carrier was clearly demonstrated. The new $3.00 passenger price for five minute rides seemed very popular as in a number of instances the same passenger remained in the ship on landing and rode as often as four times in succession."

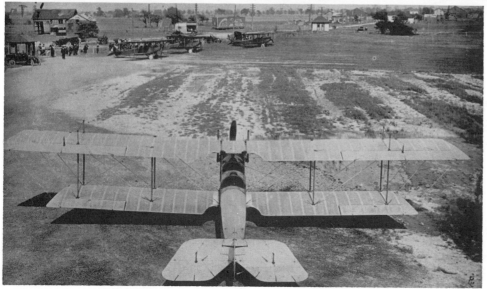

CROWD CATCHER. To entice prospective joyriders to their improvised airports, early barnstormers made spectacular flying displays. Daredevil Ron McDougal (above) clings to landing gear of Curtiss *Jenny* flying 15 feet above ground. Parachutes were scorned by these nerveless stunt men who thrilled the crowds by climbing all over their rickety, underpowered biplanes.

BARNSTORMING OPERATION (left). Typical American airport scene following World War I. Four surplus Curtiss *JN-4D Jennys* sit on edge of field, handful of curious spectators awaiting action. The *Jenny*, America's greatest contribution to the air-war effort, introduced air travel to probably more Americans than any other plane in the country.

131

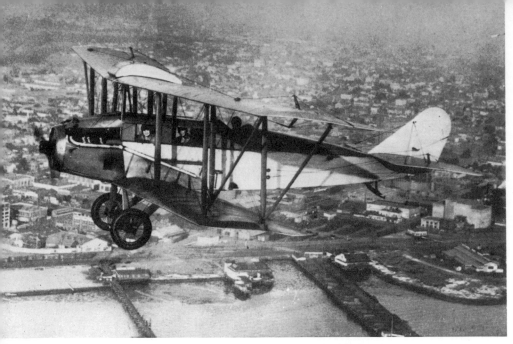

"MOST PERFECT FORM OF TRAVEL (above left) known to man," said T. Claude Ryan in advertising his Los Angeles-San Diego service, inaugurated with gestures in early Twenties. Plane was 5-place cabin "transport" used first for sightseeing. Center, Ryan Flying Company's airport in San Diego in 1926, showing fleet of *Standard* cabin biplanes and big Douglas *Cloudster*—typical airport scene of Twenties; struggling, forlorn and flanked by inevitable telephone wires.

AIRWAYS OF THE UNITED STATES—1927. Map published by Aeronautical Chamber of Commerce shows routes in operation, planned and under construction. A mere nine years after end of World War I, country had been spanned.

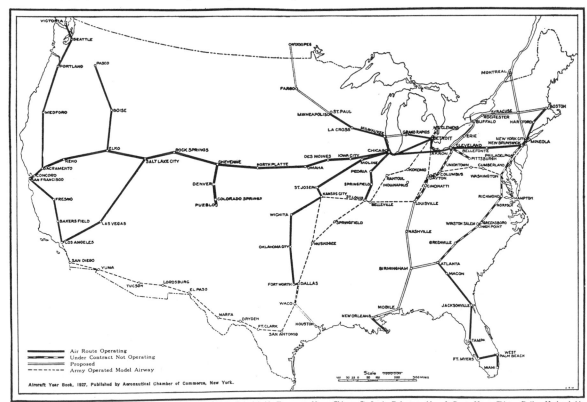

AIRWAYS OF THE UNITED STATES. No. 1, Boston-New York, Colonial Air Transport; No. 2, Chicago-St. Louis, Robertson Aircraft Corp.; No. 3, Chicago-Dallas, National Air Transport; No. 4, Salt Lake City-Los Angeles, Western Air Express; No. 5, Pasco-Elko, Walter T. Varney; No. 6, Detroit-Cleveland, Ford Motor Company; No. 7, Detroit-Chicago, Ford Motor Company; No. 8, Seattle-Los Angeles, Pacific Air Transport; No. 9, Chicago-Twin Cities, Northwest Airways; No. 10, Atlanta-Miami, Florida Airways; No. 11, Cleveland-Pittsburgh, Clifford Ball; No. 12, Cheyenne-Pueblo, Colorado Airways; No. 13, Seattle-Victoria, Edward Hubbard; No. 14, New Orleans-Pilottown, Arthur E. Cambas; No. 15, Cleveland-Louisville, Kaess Aircraft Corp.; No. 16, Detroit-Grand Rapids, Stout Air Services; No. 17, New York-Atlanta, Pitcairn Aviation; No. 18, New York-Chicago (Day), National Air Transport; No. 19, New York-Chicago (Night), National Air Transport; No. 20, Chicago-San Francisco, Boeing-Hubbard.

RYAN-CONVERTED *CLOUDSTER* built by Douglas in 1920, used by Ryan's Los Angeles-San Diego Airline in 1926. Single cabin seated 11 and passengers could move around to a limited degree. *Cloudster* was first plane to carry equivalent of its own weight.

AIRLINE PIONEER IN GOOD COMPANY (left). T. Claude Ryan, later to become famous as designer and builder of Lindbergh's "Spirit of St. Louis" and two women passengers pose in front of *Ryan-Standard* cabin biplane used on L.A.-San Diego run. At right, close-up of loading ramp and cabin of Ryan *Cloudster*.

Midwest Gets Air Service from Northwest

Northwest Orient Airlines, the second oldest air carrier in the United States with a continuous identification, began operations October 1, 1926 as an air mail carrier between Minneapolis-St. Paul and Chicago. The company was incorporated August 1, 1926 as Northwest Airways, a Michigan corporation backed by businessmen of Detroit, Minneapolis and St. Paul.

Northwest inaugurated passenger service in July 1927 with a fleet of three Stinson *Detroiters,* three-passenger cabin biplanes that cruised at 85 miles per hour. Service continued for three months before it was suspended for the winter. In 1927 the company carried 106 passengers.

In 1928 Northwest began the route expansion that saw it develop in 20 years from a small, midwestern carrier into one of the world's major domestic and international airlines that today carries over a million passengers yearly. In that year it purchased a fleet of Hamilton H-45 all-metal monoplanes to replace the then inadequate *Detroiters,* and used them for a number of years on the Minneapolis-St.Paul to Chicago route. The Hamiltons, one of the first all-metal airplanes, carried six passengers in reasonable, albeit noisy comfort, and over the years proved themselves to be highly dependable, safe planes. Powered by the 400 HP Pratt & Whitney *Wasp,* they cruised with full load at 115 miles per hour.

DEPARTURE TIME FOR SAN DIEGO — 1925. Passenger receiving "bon voyage" before takeoff in *Ryan-Standard* biplane of Los Angeles-San Diego Air Line. Note crude step for pilot and "walkaway" for passengers. Wing was definitely "No Step" area and exhaust pipe after flight was red hot, requiring use of some sort of step ladder. Pilot is seen patiently holding cabin top open while photographer snaps leave taking.

CLOUDSTER **CABIN.** Pilot's cockpit, although connected to cabin, was open. Pilots in 1926 were still reluctant to fly cooped up where they could not feel and hear rush of wind. These were "seat of the pants" flyers who kept their planes level by feel, who judged speed by sound of wind in wires, who could tell if they were slipping by breeze on either cheek.

CHICAGO BOUND. With earnest concern, Charles "Speed" Holman, Northwest Orient Airline's first pilot, watches his passengers board his *Hamilton*. One of most famous U.S. fliers during Nineteen Twenties and Thirties, Holman was killed in 1931. He still holds world's record for consecutive loop-the-loops, making 1433 in 5 hours over St. Paul airport in 1928.

NORTHWEST'S STINSON *DETROITER* used on Minneapolis-St. Paul and Chicago run in 1927—forerunner of Eddie Stinson's famous *Detroiter* monoplane, one of America's all-time great airplanes.

Boeing Extends Air Transport Service

Following Lindbergh's flight to Paris in 1927, the general attitude of the American public toward flying changed from almost complete indifference to nearly unbridled enthusiasm.

This flight, the greatest single boost aviation had ever known, cleared away the fears of flying in many a mind, and as a consequence, the demand for seats and air mail space surged upward creating a need for larger and more efficient planes.

Among the more notable planes designed to fill this requirement were the *Boeing 40s,* big, rugged biplanes designed expressly for regular transcontinental service, carrying two to four passengers in a tiny cuddy just forward of the pilot's open cockpit.

When the Post Office Department asked for bids on the San Francisco-Chicago route in 1927, Boeing, based on data collected by its Eddie Hubbard on the old pioneer Seattle-Vancouver mail run, made the lowest bid and received the contract. In five months a fleet of twenty five *40As* had been designed and built, and on July 1, 1927, Boeing pioneered the first extensive air transport service in America.

Later models of the plane, first built for Boeing Air Transport, were used by Pacific Air Transport, Western Air Express, Varney Airlines, Western Canada Airways, United Airlines and National Air Transport.

With its 400 HP Pratt & Whitney *Wasp,* the *40A* cruised at a nominal 110 miles per hour and carried two passengers in the little compartment between the cockpit and the engine, protected from the weather snug and dry, yet cramped and deafened by engine racket. The pilot, however, sitting far back in his open cockpit, enjoyed no such comforts.

The first six months of operation of Boeing's fleet of *40s* ended December 31, 1927 with a remarkable record: only five mechanical failures in 8200 hours of flying under the most extreme weather and temperature conditions. The flight schedule for these big airplanes called for a Chicago departure at 7:50 PM, arriving at Omaha at 4:30 the following morning; thence across Nebraska and Wyoming, arriving in Salt Lake City at 10:00 AM. The final leg of the trip crossed Utah and Nevada with San Francisco being reached at 4:50 PM.

The next year Boeing stepped up the power of the *40* to 525 HP and crammed in two more passengers. Known as the *40-B-A* it carried 1500 pounds of mail in addition, and cruised at 110 miles per hour.

The demand for transportation on Boeing's *40s* pointed the way for the development of something bigger and more comfortable, and in 1928 the model *80* was introduced.

This tri-motored plane, through the comfort of its passenger quarters, earned the name "Pioneer Pullman of the Air." With its fleet of *Pullmans,* Boeing Air Transport Inc., provided the longest link in the first Coast to Coast service in multi-engined planes, flying between Chicago and San Francisco on a regular schedule—as regular as the weather would allow it to be. In winter it was no fun trying to get through in snow and blizzards and low hanging clouds over the Rockies. Lacking dependable radios and accurate weather reports and all the other aids to flyers so commonplace today, it was a wonder they managed at all.

BOEINGS PACK THE MAIL. Like this one crossing the Rockies, Boeing *40-As* carried mail and passengers between San Francisco and Chicago in 1927. Payload of plane of Boeing Air Transport, predecessor of United Air Lines, was 1,000 pounds, including two passengers, mail and baggage. Cruising speed was 105 miles per hour.

The *80s* were dependable planes, lumbering and slow, but extremely stable. Their 12-place cabins were reasonably well sound-proofed, and were finished off with highly-polished mahogany. Fixtures and hardware were burnished aluminum, and each leather-upholstered seat was lighted by its own reading lamp. Aerial transportation was approaching the luxurious.

The first four of the *80* series carried 12. Eleven others built later (and powered by the more powerful *Hornet* engines) accommodated 18. But heavy mail volume seldom allowed maximum passenger loads, and generally no more than eight were carried between Chicago and Salt Lake City, and 12 on to San Francisco.

Boeing was always more than a little fussy about maintenance of its equipment, overhauling all engines at 200 hour intervals and airframes every 1,000 hours. Such attention to its planes prevented mechanical failures, and gave the line an excellent safety record which contributed immeasurably to the advancement of flying in general.

RUGGED *6,000*—**SINGLE ENGINE GREAT (above left).**
National Air Transport preferred flying mail but saw passenger opportunity in new *Travel Air* planes, flying 1,500 first year. Plane used 200 HP *Whirlwind* engine with cruising radius 600 miles. In center, Boeing's "Air Pullman," first placed in service over San Francisco-Chicago route of Boeing Air Transport, predecessor division United Air Lines.

PIONEER PULLMAN—BOEING *80* **(right)**—one of fleet providing longest link in first coast-to-coast service in multi-engined planes. *80s* were lumbering, slow but extremely stable, carried up to 18 passengers in sound-proofed comfort.

1933 MEAL ALOFT (left). Stewardess, working in narrow center aisle of Boeing *247*, serves simple fare of apples, sandwiches and coffee. In addition to great speed, *247* boasted reclining seats, a Boeing innovation. To lie back after a fine meal in overstuffed chair, soft pillow behind one's head, whisking along at 160 miles per hour—what could be better? Below, passenger quarters on one of Pacific Air Transport's Boeing *40-B-As* used on Los Angeles-Seattle run in 1928.

Then NAT Flew Passengers Too

A three place *Travel Air* monoplane was purchased in 1928 by National Air Transport, a line formed in 1925 for the exclusive business of flying the mail. Theoretically, its fleet of ten Curtiss *Carrier Pigeons* could carry an occasional passenger if need be, tucked in among the mail bags, but mail turned out to be more profitable than passengers and NAT avoided them as much as it tactfully could.

But a more or less steady trickle of passengers arriving by Boeing Air Transport into Chicago, practically forced NAT into this business, and in 1928 the new *Travel Air* went into service between Chicago and Kansas City carrying over 1500 people that year. Known among pilots simply as the *6000,* this rugged machine soon proved itself to be one of America's greatest single engined planes—so great in fact, that a number still remain in use today. An excellent load carrier, its dependable 200 horsepower *Whirlwind* gave it a cruising speed of 107 miles per hour, a radius of 600 miles and an ability to get in and out of nearly impossible areas.

RAIL PASSENGERS DELIVERED BY TRAILER-BUS. TAT *Aero Car* carried 14 persons in leather-upholstered splendor. Baggage was stored in special compartment. At each TAT station, trailer was hitched to fast car for rapid transportation between railroad station and airport.

East - West by Air - Rail

By 1929—the great boom year in aviation—America led the world in air transportation, passengers, mail and express being flown over 90,000 miles every 24 hours.

On July 4th, Transcontinental Air Transport inaugurated its cross country air-rail service, a venture costing $3 million to organize and an almost equal amount of TAT's capital to operate. Determined to provide a dependable and safe operation, TAT devised the idea of carrying its passengers by air only during daylight hours, shifting them over to the railroads at night. Total elapsed time from New York to Los Angeles ran in the neighborhood of 48 hours—not much longer than the entire trip took by train, which was still safer and cheaper.

But TAT's scheme provided glamour to the otherwise mundane business of transcontinental travel, and this proved to be its saving grace.

Leaving New York at night via Pennsylvania Railroad Pullman, the traveler arose the next morning in Columbus, Ohio where special cars shuttled him to a waiting Ford *Tri-Motor* which flew him across the flat Middle West to Waynoka, Oklahoma. Here he boarded a Santa Fe sleeper for Clovis, New Mexico where the following morning another Ford whisked him off to Los Angeles.

This was not the most convenient way to travel, perhaps, but a whole lot more dependable for the man with an unbreakable schedule than trying to make the distance entirely by air at a time when planes could be weather bound for days at a time.

The venture failed 18 months later due to a lack of Government subsidies and enough cash customers to fill the planes to anything like full capacity. What the country needed was a plane big enough and fast enough to make the trip entirely on its own, a plane capable of flying over the weather day or night.

FIRST 4-ENGINED LAND PLANES BUILT IN U.S. Five of these Fokker *F-32s* were placed in service by Western Air Express in 1929 to give public greater passenger accommodations. They carried 32, could be converted to 16-berth sleeper.

"Give Us Bigger Planes"

To meet the ever-increasing demand for a plane of greater seating capacity than then existed, Western Air Express early in 1929 placed an order with Fokker Aircraft Corp. (then a division of General Motors) for five 32-passenger transports. Designated the *F-32,* these high wing monoplanes, powered by four Pratt & Whitney *Hornets* arranged in tandem on each wing, became the first 4-engined planes built in America.

The total of 2300 HP thus generated produced a top speed of 143 miles per hour and a cruising speed of 123—a performance almost identical to the smaller *F-10* Fokker tri-motor. General construction features paralleled all Fokker aircraft—fabric-covered steel fuselage, plywood-covered wooden wings.

High up in the forward part of the fuselage sat the pilot and co-pilot in their cockpit enclosed in typical Fokker fashion by an outward-slanting windshield. Access to this domain could be made via a 3-step ladder in the cabin or through a trap door into the spacious baggage compartment beneath.

The cabin, 35 feet long, 8 feet wide and 8 feet high, accommodated its 32 passengers in four compartments separated amidship by a divided galley. This compact twin unit served light lunches and hot drinks. The entrance way, flanked by a door on either side, spanned the fuselage behind the fourth compartment. Immediately aft of this were the two washrooms.

There was nothing particularly fancy about the *F-32* interior. It could be converted into a 16-berth sleeper whenever the need arose; hot air blown through streamlined pipes between engine nacelles and fuselage warmed its passengers; individual vents at each seat provided them with abundant quantities of fresh air; a certain amount of insulation helped deaden the sound of its four great engines. But otherwise the cabin retained a pristine decor, functional, practical and weight-saving.

Imaginative and progressive Western Air Express made one attempt, however, to show what flying could be like in an *F-32,* by fitting one out in a decidedly plush manner. Tapestried walls, indirect lighting, curtains and soft divans demonstrated the maximum comfort of the *F-32* and gave a glimpse of what might be expected of future transport planes.

But the *F-32s* were born ten years too soon. Without capacity loads they could not be operated at a profit and loads of this size were difficult to come by in 1929 and 1930. This disastrous discovery, plus the fact that the U. S. Bureau of Commerce suddenly demanded regular inspections of the rot-subject wooden wings of all Fokkers (a ruinously expensive procedure), doomed these fine ships to extinction long before their time.

EXECUTIVE TRANSPORT — 1925 VERSION. Fokker *F-7* Tri-Motor laid out for business in the air. Anthony Fokker himself (in puttees) relaxes in one of ship's wicker chairs with his secretary, Helen Schunck, ready to type. Note engine controls through window of door to pilot's compartment.

MODEL DEMONSTRATES (above left) sort of comfort air travelers could expect with Western Air Express service. At right, interior of executive Fokker *10A* Tri-Motor, 1929.

SIKORSKY *S-38* IN PAN AM SERVICE (above). Between 1928 and 1930, these amphibians supplied safe, dependable transport for several domestic and foreign lines. They could climb 1,000 feet a minute fully loaded, land at 52 miles per hour.

IN AN ERA OF SPEED Lockheed *Air Express* led the flock. When Col. Roscoe Turner flew his with four passengers and baggage from Los Angeles to New York in record 19 hours including three stops, he boldly predicted transcontinental air service within few years. Introduced in 1928, plane had notable installation of new engine cowling developed for Lockheed *Vega,* was also first plane equipped with "pants" on landing gear.

Sikorsky Amphibians Add Safety

Western Air Express, later known as Transcontinental and Western Air, or TWA, and more recently called Trans World Airlines with the same initials, began operations as a mail carrier in April 1926, flying an established route between Salt Lake City and Los Angeles.

Within two years it had expanded operations to express and passenger-carrying between Pueblo, Colorado Springs, Denver and Cheyenne, and one Lockheed *Air Express,* the fastest passenger plane of the day. Carrying four and their baggage, this graceful high-wing monoplane cruised at 150 miles per hour.

Western also operated a service between Los Angeles and Catalina Island, a line purchased from Pacific Marine Airways, which had operated World War I surplus Curtiss *HS2L* flying boats across the 26 miles of water for over five years without an accident. A Sikorsky *S-38* amphibian was added to the fleet of *HS-2Ls* offering a faster service because of its increased speed and its ability to taxi onto ramps, thereby speeding loading and unloading operations. This machine provided probably the safest aerial transportation known at the time, for the combination of twin engines and the ability to operate from land or sea is a most conducive one to trouble-free flying.

The *S-38* was the largest and fastest amphibian in the world when Sikorsky introduced it in 1928. A pair of 400 HP *Wasps* gave it a top speed of 129 miles per hour and a safe landing speed of 52. The passenger cabin, with seats for nine to thirteen depending on the distances to be flown, was 9 feet 3 inches long, 5 feet wide and 51 inches high, and its wicker chairs were fastened to the floor with turnbuckles. Gray artificial leather covered walls and ceiling. Trim was mahogany. For seaworthiness, windows remained fixed, but ventilators provided an ample amount of air.

This ship performed amazingly well, climbing a thousand feet a minute fully loaded, cruising at 110 miles per hour, and possessing an ability to maintain altitude on a single engine. Over a hundred of these machines were built by Sikorsky between 1928 and 1930, seeing service on domestic and foreign airlines: PAA, Pan American Grace, Inter-Island Airways, Canadian Colonial Airways, NYRBA, to name a few. It was a tremendously rugged and safe plane, and conservative estimates place the total mileage accumulated on all *S-38s* at better than 25,000,000, or roughly a thousand times around the world.

"THANK YOU, NURSE." Pioneer air hostess pours coffee on Boeing Air Transport *Pullman*. Public and crew members loved this new personalized service.

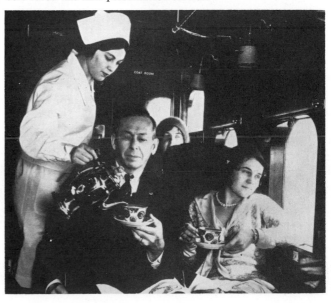

BRANIFF'S FIRST (above left). 5-place 90 miles per hour Stinson *Detroiter* flew three round trips daily between Tulsa and Oklahoma City in 1928. Center, passengers embarking on Eastern Air *Condor* at Washington Airport for New York, 1929. Dirt and grass field was far cry from Washington's present facilities.

Braniff Bridges the Oil Country

Braniff International Airways, today one of the country's largest airlines, serving the entire midwestern section of the U. S. and linked to South America, began operations on June 20, 1928 flying between Oklahoma City and Tulsa. A five passenger 90 mile-an-hour Stinson *Detroiter* powered by a 220 HP Wright *Whirlwind* engine flew three round trips daily along the 116 mile route, providing a dependable and extensively used service between these two cities.

Before the year ended, Braniff had added a second *Detroiter,* a pair of Travelair monoplanes and a Ryan. With 16 people on the payroll including six pilots, the line carried 3000 people during the first six months of operation without a serious accident.

Today one of Braniff's Boeing *707* jets could fly the original Oklahoma City-Tulsa route in 11 minutes with 23 times as many passengers.

SLEEPING ACCOMMODATIONS (left) on American Airlines' *Condor*—service began Feb. 16, 1936. At right, another interior view of *Condor.*

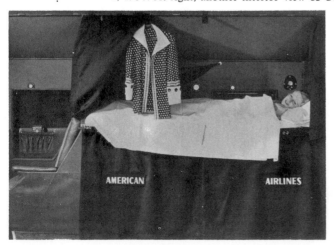

NINE TON *CONDOR* **FLIES FOR EASTERN.** Big biplane provided comfort-plus to 18 passengers largely through elimination of noisy, smelly nose engine.

Curtiss Launches CONDOR

Early in the summer of 1929 Curtiss Aeroplane and Engine Company entered the large passenger transport field with its *Condor,* at that time one of the largest planes to be built in America.

With a wing spread of 91 feet, 8 inches and a gross weight of 9 tons, this big biplane carried 18 passengers and a crew of two. Its cabin, long and wide and with 6 feet 8 inches of headroom, was divided into three compartments: six reclining seats in two of them—lounge seats in the other. A lavatory between the forward two contained the usual plumbing fixtures, plus hot and cold running water.

Curtiss exerted every effort to make the *Condor* a truly comfortable plane for its passengers. Windows were large for full visibility. Each seat had its own reading light and a serving tray was easily attached to its arms. A hot water heating system that utilized small boilers on the engine exhaust manifolds provided warmth, while an ample ventilating system supplied fresh air. Smart fabrics decorated overhead and walls, while grain leather was used on seats and mahogany formica on partitions and trim.

Because there was no engine on the nose of the *Condor,* the cabin was free from the vibration and noise, the heat and smell that characterized trimotored planes. Sound proofing of the cabin and the use of 3-bladed propellers turning at half speed materially reduced engine noise. Experiments by Sperry Gyroscope Co. on sound proofing of the *Condor* paid off handsomely for Curtiss, tests indicated conclusively that the decibel count showed 75—exactly the same as that of a Pullman car. By way of comparison, the Ford Tri-Motors proved to be a whopping 105.

A pair of 12 cylinder Curtiss *Conqueror* water cooled engines, chosen in preference to air cooled ones because of their substantially greater power and proven reliability, powered the *Condor.* Flight could be maintained on either one. As an added safety feature each nacelle was furnished with a CO_2 fire extinguisher, operated from the cockpit.

So dependable and economical to operate were these first *Condors,* that five were still being used by Eastern as late as August 1933. By this time Curtiss had produced a newer and faster model, powered by a pair of 700 HP Wright *Cyclones.* The greater horse power and lighter weight of these engines plus retracting landing gears helped boost the speed of these machines to better than 170 miles per hour—20 miles per hour faster than other multi-engined transports of the day.

With its fleet of *Condors,* American Airlines inaugurated a high speed service between Chicago and New York, making the trip in a little more than 5½ hours. Eastern's *Condors* established a 95 minute service between New York and Washington, while others of its fleet flew regularly between New York and Miami. It was a good wholesome airplane with no great faults, and was used both as a day plane and as a sleeper by Eastern. In its heyday it boasted the lowest operating cost per seat mile of any multi-engine transport in service.

As late as 1941 at least six *Condors* were still in operation, China National Airways, an affiliate of Pan American Airways, having bought them from a California junkman. Along with some *DC3s* and *DC2s,* this line flew over 2000 miles a day under war time conditions.

Henry Ford's "Tin Goose"

The Ford *Tri-Motor,* used by all the major airlines throughout the United States during the late Nineteen Twenties and early Thirties, proved to be one of the most durable planes ever built. In spite of the fact production ceased in 1932 dozens of the original 199 constructed remained in service for years after, and as late as January 1958, at least 11 were registered and still flying in the United States.

The *Tri-Motor* represented an attempt by Henry Ford to apply automobile production line methods to airplane building. The basic design was frozen in 1926, although minor modifications were made from time to time—all of them designed to improve this great ship's performance.

It was not a heavy plane, for Ford engineers realized the great penalties imposed on performance by weight. Compared with the lumbering Handley Pages, and Argosys then in use on British routes, it was a featherweight. It grossed 5000 pounds less than its nearest rival, the Boeing *80.* But it possessed great strength and imposed few if any maintenance problems. Thanks to this weight-saving it outperformed all the world's transports in speed, range and economy of operation.

Known affectionately as the "Tin Goose", this 11 to 15 passenger high wing monoplane flew easily and could carry big loads in and out of impossibly small fields. This feature, probably more than any other, accounts for its continued popularity down through the years, especially by freight line operators.

Ford concentrated production on the two standard airline models—the *4-ATs* and *5-ATs.* These two differed basically only in wing span and power: 74 feet and 660 HP for the former and 77 feet and 1280 HP for the latter. Although the larger engines added 700 pounds of weight, their extra power increased the useful load from 3650 pounds to 6000, while adding five miles per hour to the cruising speed.

Under light load conditions either model could maintain altitude with one engine out, but under normal airline conditions, the remaining two engines could be counted on only to stretch its glide.

Ford spared no effort in making the *Tri-Motor* the greatest plane in the world, but minimum passenger comfort (on the earliest models, at least) was considered adequate. Although later models provided some semblance of luxury, the *Tri-Motor* remained a purely functional aircraft designed to get people to their destinations and back with the least fuss and pampering and in the greatest possible safety.

The earliest models were furnished with plain wicker seats. Simple baggage racks overhead, along with a few ceiling lights, completed the meagre furnishings. Walls were lined with a drab colored composite paper insulation, elaborately called "Ford Aeroboard," which did little or nothing to keep engine noises out of the cabin. Later models were somewhat more plush, with pillow headrests on each seat, window curtains, individual electric reading lights, lavatory with hot and cold water, braided silk hand grips for support in rough air, and cabin heaters. And the general finish of the overhead and walls was noticeably more bright and cheery.

In a grand effort to sell his product, Ford ran full page advertisements in national magazines praising the *Tri-Motors:* "Room for Twelve . . . and their baggage" ran the lead on one. "1,000,000 Miles. . . . Stout Air Lines" read another. "How Big? How Small?" asked a third. "Does it seem fanciful to suggest that transport operators will need planes capable of carrying 12 passengers and their baggage?". Such advertising did much to sell the public on aerial transportation and Ford airplanes as well.

By the end of 1929 Stout Air Lines, operating between Detroit, Chicago and Cleveland, had carried over a hundred thousand passengers in its fleet of

ON THE LINE

NOT OFTEN does the National Air Transport assemble its fleet of Ford tri-motored, all-metal planes, because, like a railroad, the "rolling stock" must keep moving. Every hour day and night an N. A. T. plane is humming through the skies on its scheduled way, carrying cargo of passengers, mail or express.

The fleet of fourteen-passenger transports is pictured here about to take its place with the famous fliers of the United Air Lines, of which National Air Transport is one of the most active divisions. You can properly imagine each of these perfectly groomed machines taking off to a different destination over established lines, guided by electric beacons, controlled from point to point by radio telegraph and telephone.

Their goals might be: New York . . . Dallas . . . Toledo . . . Fort Worth . . . Cleveland . . . Tulsa . . . Chicago . . . Moline . . . Kansas City . . . Oklahoma.

From all these points the National Air Transport can today make swift connection with sister air-lines flying to all important centers west of the Mississippi. You can now fly by National Air Transport, without stop-overs, from the Atlantic to the Pacific in 31 hours; and from the Pacific to the Atlantic in 28 hours.

Five years' experience in transport flying and eleven million miles of successful operation are the foundation of this necessary transportation service.

Of course, Ford all-metal, tri-motored commercial transports form an important part of the National Air Transport fleet. For Ford planes are in demand wherever the American public has learned to accept aviation as a commercial factor of importance.

Last year alone Ford planes flew 8,000,000 miles!

FORD MOTOR COMPANY

"8,000,000 MILES LAST YEAR." Ford Motor Company advertisement in 1931 issue of "Aviation."

"ROOM FOR TWELVE . . . AND THEIR BAGGAGE" ran the caption on one of series of advertisements by Ford under this photo of *Tri-Motor.* "Does it seem fanciful to suggest that transport operators will need planes capable of carrying 12 passengers and their baggage? Does it seem unlikely planes of this capacity can be filled?"

Tri-Motors without the slightest injury to anyone and by June of the following year this line was flying four round trips a day between Detroit, Toledo and Cleveland. The same year Transcontinental Air Transport inaugurated the first all-air coast to coast service, making the westbound flight in 28 hours; the eastbound in 24½. In all, 95 companies used *Tri-Motors* on scheduled and non-scheduled passenger service throughout the world.

Ford digressed somewhat from its policy of building standardized models only when it introduced the *de luxe Club Model* in 1930. Advertised as a "winged yacht, beautiful as a jewel, comfortable as your club", this standard *5-AT* carried nine in celestial splendor at a cruising speed of 122 MPH.

It contained a kitchenette, folding berths, radio cabinet, writing desk and card tables. There was a bookcase, seven overstuffed chairs, a divan for two, serving trays, refrigerator and thermos bottles. Walls and ceilings were most effectively soundproofed and the lavatory was complete with running water.

The interior was "beautifully trimmed and decorated in choice fabrics". There were dome lights and wall lights, ventilators at every window and heat registers in the floor. Walls in the lavatory and kitchenette were lined with tile.

Equipped with every device known at the time for day and night flying in all seasons under most normal conditions, the *Club Model,* even by today's standards, was an exceptionally comfortable and safe plane.

HENRY FORD'S *TRI-MOTOR* **TRIUMPH** "Tin Goose," used by all major airlines in U.S. in Twenties and Thirties, proved highly durable over the years. A comparative "featherweight" it flew easily, could carry big loads out of small fields, helped to sell public on aerial travels.

TRAVEL IN MEXICO (below left). Ford *5-AT-B Tri-Motor* owned by Compania Mexicana de Aviacion in 1931, offered patrons most modern transport equipment then in use—and by far most convenient. At right, Mexican steward awaits arrival of passengers. Note receiver radio to his left, distinct innovation for 1931.

HAND GRIPS BUT NO SAFETY BELTS. Ford *Tri-Motor* cabin complete with pillow head rests, window curtains, electric reading lights.

BITE IN FLIGHT. Sandwiches and cold drinks were luxuries aloft in 1928 on this Ford tri-motored plane on Chicago-New York route of National Air Transport, predecessor company of United Air Lines.

149

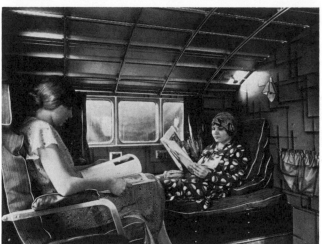

NIGHT FLIGHT (above). Passengers board "Midnight Flyer," United Air Lines Ford *Tri-Motor* for midnight-to-breakfast trip, New York to Chicago. By end of 1929, 10,358 miles of country's principal airways were lighted sufficiently to allow around-the-clock passenger service New York-California, up and down both coasts. Facilities consisted of over 275 lighted airports and emergency fields, 1,352 rotating beacons.

AFTER CABIN CONSOLIDATED *COMMODORE* offered colorful comfort to high degree.

Flying Down to Rio

A year or so before any interest in South America had been displayed by Pan American, the New York, Rio and Buenos Aires Air Line Inc. NYRBA began flying between these cities using a fleet of 12 twin engine Consolidated *Commodore* flying boats, the largest commercial seaplanes to have been built in numbers in America at the time.

The *Commodore* was a central hull monoplane powered by a pair of Pratt & Whitney *Hornets* rated at 575 HP each. Its wings spanned 100 feet, it was 61 feet long and it grossed 17,600 pounds.

Actually this fine big seaplane was a commercial adaptation of the XPY-1 *Admiral* Naval patrol bomber, grandpappy of the PBY boats used so extensively before World War II and during its early years.

Its cabin was 8 feet 5 inches wide with 6 foot headroom and was entered through the mail storage compartment located in the extreme after end of the hull. Immediately ahead of this were three passenger compartments with large windows on each side. The first contained two seats and two daybeds; the second and third were furnished with double seats facing each other on either side of the aisle. A wash room to port and a radio room to starboard separated these passenger compartments from the pilot's in the bow —open in the first model but closed in subsequent ones. Laid out in this manner the *Commodore* carried 20 passengers.

BIG SEAPLANE OVER ATLANTIC on South American run originated by New York, Rio and Buenos Aires Air Line Inc. Twelve of these twin-engine Consolidated *Commodore* flying boats were used, each carrying twenty passengers.

The prototype was outstanding in finish and design, somewhat more elaborate than standard models used by NYRBA on its jungle runs. The motif featured tropical colors—silver, henna and green. Damask-covered walls decorated the two forward compartments, while a pale lavender and silver Deauville repp material was used in the deluxe "salon". Turquoise damask seat cushions trimmed with gold-, raspberry- and tan-striped cloth adorned the daybeds here, while lemon-yellow and tan draperies hung in the windows, and jade-green rugs carpeted the center aisle. All in all the *Commodore* cabin was little short of lush.

Each compartment contained a rack for magazines and papers, a removable Pullman-type card or writing table, and individual electric lights.

NYRBA, unable to obtain sufficiently large mail contracts from the Government, its backers scared off by the great depression, and faced with the stiffest kind of competition, in 1930 merged with its biggest competitor, Pan American Airways.

The new owners enlarged the *Commodore* fleet to 20, flying them from Miami over the West Indies and the East Coast route to Buenos Aires—a 9000 mile route touching 15 countries on an amazingly efficient and regular schedule.

FULL LOAD FOR CHICAGO. Passengers on National Air Transport Ford *Tri-Motor* await takeoff. Note speedometer and altimeter on forward bulkheads. Coats and hats point up lack of heat.

151

NYRBA *COMMODORE* **LANDS EASILY (above).** Consolidated *Fleetster* below, used in desperation attempt by NYRBA in South America to speed air mail delivery, had top speed of 175 miles per hour powered by Pratt & Whitney *Wasp*. *Fleetster* land planes were used extensively in 1932 and 1933 by Ludington Airlines, Inc. on high speed service between New York, Philadelphia, Washington every hour on the hour, carrying pilot and eight passengers.

FLEETSTER **ON LUDINGTON'S RUN (below)** although mainstay was fleet of Stinson tri-motors. Ludington was one of few lines of day to operate at profit without Government air mail contracts, thanks to strict economy measures.

Biggest Amphibians For Jungle Routes

In spite of the depression that swept the country in 1929, the demand for aerial transportation continued to grow almost unabated. Probably the "growingest" line in the world at the time was Pan American Airways with its Caribbean and South American operation. Its routes stretched from Brownsville to Mexico City, from Miami to Cuba across Yukatan, down Central America to Panama and South America, from Miami to Puerto Rico. By the end of the year it owned 44 planes, employed 1200 people and operated from 71 airports.

Its scheduled efficiency was 99.65% in spite of the fact that great portions of its routes stretched over water and across the treacherous jungles and mountain ranges of Guatemala, Mexico and Central America. It was the most difficult sort of flying but it was also the most lucrative, because here in this primitive portion of the world where the ox cart ruled supreme, the airplane opened new frontiers as had the early railroads of the Far West. The demand for transportation exceeded the supply of seats and Pan Am turned to the idea of building bigger, faster and longer-range aircraft.

By 1930 a contract had been awarded Sikorsky Aircraft for a long-range seaplane and in August 1931 the prototype has been successfully tested. The *S-40* was a marvel of aeronautical engineering. Not only was it the biggest plane that had ever been constructed in America but it was the largest amphibian in the world. It was an awkward looking ship, with its four engines slung below the wings (the advantage of placing power plants in the wing's leading edge had not yet been discovered), but it surpassed anything Pan American had used before and its multi-engine feature held great passenger appeal. Furthermore it carried better than four tons of payload.

With 40 passengers and a ton of cargo its range was 500 miles. With 24 people, the range stretched to 950. Cruising speed with its four Pratt and Whitney *Hornets* developing a total of 2300 HP averaged 115 miles per hour. It could fly easily on any three engines.

Although used primarily as a flying boat, the *S-40* carried wheels as an added safety feature for the 50 mile hop across Cuba. It may be difficult to understand the reasoning behind the decision to carry 1700 pounds of deadweight across 1300 miles of ocean until one remembers that this was pioneering of the first order. Pan American was taking no chances.

With this big ship the torturous dog leg flight to Panama was eliminated and shaved 650 miles off the trip by flying directly across the Caribbean to Barranquilla, stopping only at Jamaica. Transocean flying had begun in earnest and in a most luxurious manner, for seaplanes were renowned for their comfort.

A flying boat hull required a displacement sufficiently great to float its own weight plus that of its wings and engines, its fuel, its passengers and cargo, and for this reason it was necessarily larger than the fuselage of a land plane with similar flight characteristics. And because it had to withstand the tremendous shocks of rough water landings, and contain watertight bulkheads and other special equipment, it was a far more rugged structure. This increase in size and strength unfortunately meant a gain in weight which in turn reduced carrying capacity—a loss for the operator but a boon for the passengers who rattled around in the vast expanse of hull in a degree of comfort never known before.

And so it was with the *S-40* cabin which was 18 inches wider than a Pullman car. It was divided into eight spacious compartments with wide aisles between and up to eight feet of headroom. There was a buffet and a smoking room, a ladies' lounge and three chair compartments with a superb view from each of the big opening windows.

The walls were paneled with walnut and draperies of heavy silk decorated the windows. The chairs were gaily upholstered in blue and orange and beside each was an ash tray, electric light, cigarette lighter and call button for the steward.

Three *S-40s* were built for Pan American: *American Clipper, Southern Clipper* and *Caribbean Clipper* and saw service steadily from 1932 to 1943 whereupon they joined the War effort doing navigation training for the Navy.

By the early Thirties all the world's great oceans had been flown—but only by planes especially rigged for the trips, jammed shoe-horn tight with fuel tanks and seldom carrying more than two people.

The vast oceans that separated the United States from Europe on one side, and Asia and Australia on the other, stretched too far to be spanned by any large passenger-carrying planes of the day. No commercial plane then in existence could carry a payload more than six or seven hundred miles non-stop—far too little range for the Atlantic and Pacific.

For these long hops bigger and heavier planes were needed, planes that could carry cash customers in addition to the thousands of gallons of gasoline required for the long flights. But larger planes meant bigger airports with extended runways strong enough to support their great weight and few countries felt inclined to expend large sums of money to build them for the limited amount of traffic that logically could be expected. The seaplane, with its ability to land practically anywhere on the globe, was obviously the machine for the job.

Scarcely had the *S-40* entered service than Pan American announced its needs for a bigger and faster airplane—something that could take the oceans in stride. Its requirements staggered the country's builders: a 2500 mile non-stop cruising range at 145 miles per hour with 12 passengers and crew! Only Martin and Sikorsky accepted the challenge, a challenge that required a whole new approach to aeronautical design, for only radical changes could produce such a plane.

Sikorsky completed its plane first, delivering an *S-42* (then the largest seaplane in the world) in the Fall of 1934. Powered by a quartet of Pratt & Whitney *Hornets* developing 700 HP apiece, this sleek flying boat cruised at 160 miles per hour—15 more than Pan American required. Its top speed exceeded 175. It carried 32 passengers and five crew members on short-haul jaunts but its radius, even with a dozen passengers, fell far short of Pan Am's requirements. Nevertheless, the *S-42* proved to be a marvellous airplane and provided sure-fire, comfortable service between New York and Bermuda, Miami and South America, Manila and Hong Kong, and equipped with extra tanks to extend its radius over 3000 miles (without passengers), it flew survey flights across both Atlantic and Pacific.

Flush riveting, flaps, streamlining, leading edge-mounted engines, all contributed toward making the *S-42*'s performance vastly superior to the *S-40*. Its hull contained nine watertight compartments: anchor locker, pilot's cockpit, baggage room, four passenger cabins each with eight chairs, lavatories and entrance way.

ONE ANSWER TO CHALLENGE. Pan American Airways demanded plane to conquer the ocean and Sikorsky answered with the *S-42*. Four P & W *Hornets* developed 700 HP each, ship cruised at 160 miles per hour with top speed over 175.

The Martin M-130

Martin's answer to Pan American's requirements was the giant *M-130*—a 52,000 pound flying boat capable of carrying 12 passengers 3000 miles non-stop—a distressingly low ratio of payload to size by today's standards but remarkable in 1936.

Pan American inaugurated its Pacific service with the *M-130* on October 21, 1936. Island hopping from Alameda, California to Manila, the *M-130s* covered the distance in an average of 60 hours flying time providing previously unknown comforts for their minute compliments of passengers. And at each stopping point—Hawaii, Midway, Wake, Guam—Pan Am furnished them with neat, modern quarters for overnight stays, for this was before the days of one-stop Pacific flying.

The *M-130* resembled the *S-42* only generally. Both planes were 4-engined, high wing flying boats;

both were all metal. But here all resemblances ended, for the *M-130* surpassed the Sikorsky in all departments: speed, size, carrying ability and range.

Its main cabin, nearly 45 feet long, contained overstuffed settees (convertible into berths) for 18 people, an efficient and complete galley, lounge complete with bookcase, table and desks, twin lavatories, and in the extreme end of the fuselage, quarters for three crew members. It was a far cry from today's high density transports carrying 80 to 120 people crammed into their seats with little or no freedom of movement. The seaplane traveler of 1936 may have taken longer to cover a given distance between two points but he did it in a style and degree of spaciousness probably never again to be enjoyed by any aerial passengers.

BOEING *314 CLIPPER*

On June 21, 1936 Pan American Airways signed a three million dollar contract with Boeing Aircraft Company for six giant flying boats. Known as the *314 Clippers* they were the largest and most famous seaplanes ever built. By early 1939 Pan Am had begun regular trans-Pacific service with them, and before the year ended, ordered six more.

The *314* accommodated 74 day passengers (40 at night) in addition to its eight man crew. Four 1700 HP 18 cylinder Wright *Cyclones* carried its total weight of 84,000 pounds for a maximum range of 5200 miles at a cruising speed of 184 miles per hour.

It was a superb plane by any standards, past or present, and became the first to operate profitably on the long over-ocean routes. Only World War II with its cold demands for speed brought about its obsolescence well before its time.

It was the most comfortable and luxurious plane ever built. Its hull was divided into two decks connected by a spiral staircase (an arrangement used by Boeing ten years later on its *Stratocruisers*.) The upper deck contained the control room forward (a space that measured 12 feet by 21 feet) occupied by the pilot and co-pilot, the navigator, radio operator, flight engineer and captain. Aft of this, in the area where the massive wings joined the hull, was a vast cargo space, and behind this the crew quarters, for the *Clippers* carried extra men on the long ocean flights.

The lower deck was divided into a number of ten-passenger compartments for day travel—six for night—a dining and lounging area amidship and a deluxe compartment aft. There were commodious wash rooms for men and women, and an extremely complete galley served full course meals.

FAMOUS IN THE EARLY THIRTIES. One of Braniff's fleet of Lockheed *Vegas,* noted for its rugged dependability and speed. Some 130 of these beautiful ships were built, approximately half dozen surviving to this day.

PAN AMERICAN'S *S-40* **AMPHIBIAN WAS MARVEL** of engineering (above left), biggest plane ever constructed in America, carrying 4 tons of payload—40 passengers and ton of cargo —500 miles, cruising at 115 miles per hour. Four Pratt & Whitney *Hornet* engines developed 2300 HP. Center, is *M-130,* second answer to Pan American. Fifty-two thousand pounds of flying boat surpassed *S-42* in size, speed, carrying ability and range. Carried 12 passengers 3,000 miles non-stop. At right, 6800 HP pulls magnificent Boeing *Clipper* off water into its natural element.

All four engines could be reached in flight through a tunnel in the wing, allowing minor repairs if required. Any two engines could keep the *314* airborne.

Boeing built two series of six aircraft apiece. Two of the first six were used on the Pacific and four on the Atlantic. Two of the second six were ordered on September 12, 1939 and the first was delivered in May, 1941. The British Government bought the first two of this group, the United States taking the third. Pan American retained the remaining three. These were taken off scheduled runs with great frequency during War years to undertake special secret missions to many parts of the world, both on and off PAA's commercial routes. To chronicle them, a book on this subject alone would be required, and many of their journeys and passenger lists are still restricted information.

One *314* was forced down in mid-Atlantic some years after the War, on a non-scheduled flight, when strong head winds exhausted its fuel supply. Although hampered by tremendous seas, all 80 passengers were saved, thanks to the great sea-keeping ability of the Boeing hull and the daring seamanship of members of the rescuing Coast Guard vessel.

So far as is known, none of the original 12 *Clippers* exists today. With the huge upsurge in aerial travel following World War II, the demand for faster, more economical land planes quickly antiquated these splendid ships and they soon joined the swelling ranks of obsolescent aircraft the world over.

And so ended the era of the great seaplanes. The vast network of airports built up throughout the world during the War made trans-ocean flying by multi-engined land planes completely feasible. Freed from the restrictions of carrying dead-weight seagoing hulls on their over-water planes, designers and builders turned to the creation of highly efficient land planes capable of spanning oceans in a fraction of the Clippers' times.

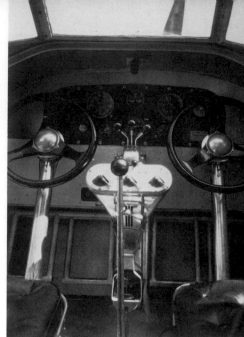

BIGGEST SEAPLANE DISCHARGES PAYLOAD. Boeing *314 Clippers* were the most famous ever built. Carrying 74 day passengers (40 over-night and 8 man crew)—84,000 pounds at 184 miles per hour over 5,200 mile range—they proved superb by any standards.

SENSATION FROM THE START (above). Pennsylvania Central Airlines' Boeing *247s* such as this provided speed, safety, comfort hitherto unknown. Twin 550 *Wasps* gave it cruising speed of 180 miles per hour, far faster than any commercial plane then, and newly invented Hamilton Standard controllable pitch propellers could pull it up to almost unheard of ceiling of 27,000 feet—a wonder plane of the age. Below, New York and Suburban Airlines' Bellanca *Aircruiser* docking at Wall Street Skyport. 700 HP Wright *Cyclone*-powered 10-passenger plane carried more than 1,000 Wall Streeters to and from homes in Port Washington, Glen Cove, Oyster Bay on daily flights from July 17 to Sept. 28, 1934.

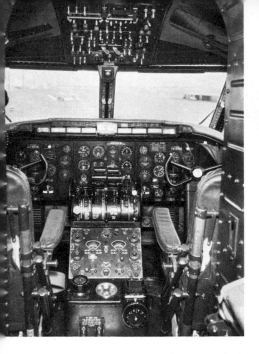

METAMORPHOSIS (two center photos above). Rapid development in aeronautical control is here contrasted. In only 15 years the wonderful simplicity of Ford *Tri-Motor* gave way to complexities of post-war airliner. Ford panel contained only speedometer, altimeter, turn indicator, clock and three instruments for nose engine. Instruments for outboard engines were mounted on panels immediately behind cylinders visible from pilots' seats through side windows.

GANGWAY STRADDLED GAP (above right) between loading float and *314's* port sponson. Boeing built 12 for over 6 million dollars. Hull was divided into two decks connected by spiral staircase—crew and control rooms above, cargo aft, passenger area below.

TWENTY YEARS OF PROGRESS. In 1949 Trans World Airlines dramatized its 20th year of coast-to-coast flying by putting a sleek *Constellation* (below) and Ford *Tri-Motor* in air at same time.

Douglas Introduces the DCs

Early in 1934 Donald Douglas introduced the *DC-2,* a brand new model with a performance superior to anything in the air at the time. Flown from coast-to-coast that year in a record-shattering 13 hours and four minutes, it served notice on all other transport planes of the day—the *247*s, the *80*s, the Fords, the Fokkers—that another era of aerial transportation had arrived.

Here was a plane operators had been waiting and praying for, a plane with all the earmarks of a genuine money maker. Orders piled up in the Douglas factory and over a hundred were built. But the best was yet to come, for a year later Douglas brought out the *DC-3,* a plane destined to become the most popular transport ever created.

There is no question that the *DC-3* did more for the advancement of commercial aviation than any single plane ever built. When placed in regular transcontinental service it slashed flying times in half, boosting ticket sales to all time highs. For here was an airplane able to carry 21 passengers at 180 miles per hour through and above the weather in comfort and incomparable safety. By 1939 *DC-3*s were used on virtually every scheduled airline in the world.

The plane was a natural from the start, easy to fly, forgiving of pilot errors, aerodynamically sound. It was one of the first transport planes to be built entirely of metal and it was also one of the first to possess a retractable landing gear. Its ruggedness gave it an unparalleled life span, thousands of the original 11,000 built remaining in active service today. Its ability to get in and out of small, unpaved fields has been unmatched by any present day planes of comparable size. No manufacturer has come up with the perfect plane to "replace the *DC-3*" and having survived the onslaught of the great transports of the 1940s and 1950s, it appears perfectly capable of holding its own in the jet age.

FIRST OF ROYAL LINE—*DC-2*. In 1934 Donald Douglas introduced a brand new model with superior performance. It made coast-to-coast records that presaged a new day in commercial flight.

To A Lovely Lady!

Comfortable?

Please don't change your position just now. There is too much out the window that you would otherwise be missing...and we know it is so restful sitting that way...while you relax in the deep upholstery of your lounge chair.

Smoke, if you care to...or read with the little light that shines over your shoulder and just on your book. Or perhaps the wide aisle may invite you to a brief stroll down the long cabin.

Everything is quiet and the smart simplicity of the appointments suit you perfectly. Although your destination may be on the other side of America, you seem very much at home. Indeed we hope so, for that will give us the satisfaction of knowing you, too, have enjoyed your journey aboard a Douglas Air Transport.

Douglas Aircraft Company, Inc., Santa Monica, California

YOU, BACK AT HOME—RELAX TOO. Advertisements like this one of Douglas Aircraft Company's *DC-3s* did much to stimulate interest in aerial transportation in mid-Thirties.

DC-6 **CIRCLING OVER MEXICO CITY.** The "6" entered scheduled airline service in 1947, has served over 25 airlines in all parts of globe. Although surpassed in speed, carrying capacity and efficiency by more modern airliners, DC-6s still form an important part of many major airlines' stables. Seating capacity varies from 54 to 89 with cruising radius on extended range models stretching out to 5,000 miles.

GRAND OLD LADY OF AIRWAYS: SABENA *DC-3s* on the line in Belgium—most popular transport ever built—easy to fly, forgiving of pilot error, aerodynamically sound. It slashed flying time and boosted ticket sales, could carry 21 passengers and baggage at 180 miles per hour through and above the weather.

ALL ASHORE. Passengers disembark from New York and Suburban's Bellanca *Aircruiser* on Skyport's ramp few blocks from their downtown New York offices. One secret of Bellanca's great carrying capacity (this was largest single-engined plane in world at time) was manner in which all bracing struts were aerofoil-shaped for extra lift. This peculiarity of design is most evident in this photograph.

FORERUNNER OF TRANS-OCEAN AIRLINERS. Douglas *DC-4,* one of most dependable planes ever built, used on majority of world's airlines, scheduled and nonscheduled, always a favorite with pilots because of handling ease. Average *DC-4* seats 42, cruises at 200 miles per hour, weighs 65,000 pounds gross.

BOEING MONOMAIL OF 1930. This six passenger low wing monoplane, first designed as an all-cargo ship, later modified to combination passenger-cargo service, was first truly revolutionary Boeing plane. Its development led to *B-9* bombers and *247* transport.

All duralumin skin cut maintenance and increased safety. Wing was internally braced—probably the first plane in America to be built minus struts and bracing wires. Its landing gear was retracted—a definite innovation for 1930.

Monomail proved to be fastest and most streamlined plane built up until then in America but it carried less than Boeing *80* and design work shifted to creation of the amazing Boeing *247*—father of all present day commercial transports.

FINISHING TOUCHES. A parent buttons his son's coat before boarding New Zealand Airways DC-3.

LOCKHEED *ELECTRA* **IN 1934**—flown by Braniff Airways—12 place ship, popular with airlines, corporations and individual owners over the world.

The Lockheed ELECTRA

When *Electra* was introduced by Lockheed in 1934, it was the only plane produced in America with an all-metal external surface. It was also Lockheed's first model to have multiple vertical tail surfaces which came to identify later Lockheed aircraft.

Other features included 2-way controllable propellers, electrically operated flaps, hydraulic brakes and dual controls. The *Electra* was a 12-place ship, popular with airlines, corporations and private owners throughout the world.

An apple, ham sandwich and hunk of chocolate cake, with or without coffee—depending on whether the pilot happened to bring any along—was the in-flight meal to which Braniff Airways' passengers were treated on "express" flights in the early Thirties.

The first airplane of this model built in 1934 was still being operated by the Department of National Defense in Ottawa, according to a recent check.

The need for fast and efficient transportation of military and Government personnel and key defense industry employees during World War II taxed the world's airlines almost beyond their capacity. In the

United States alone, the number of passengers carried by domestic airlines jumped from 2,959,480 in 1940 to an unprecedented 4,060,545 in 1941. By the time the war had ended, the figure reached 7,502,538. Travel was strictly by priority, and John Q. Public took very much a back seat, flying only when no personage of greater importance needed a ride.

Mainstay of the airlines during these hectic years was the dependable old *DC-3* and its big brother, the 4-engined *DC-4,* predecessor of the modern trans-ocean air liner. By 1943 Lockheed had introduced its mighty *Constellation* which went into production on a grand scale the following year. Designed to cross the United States in under nine hours, this 8800 HP giant could carry 62 passengers and a crew of five at better than 300 miles per hour. These three and the big load-carrying Curtiss-Wright *C-46 Commando* carried the brunt of the world's aerial cargoes —men, machines, wounded, refugees, soldiers, paratroopers—practically everything that needed transporting.

166

LIGHTER THAN AIR

There can be little question that the most luxurious and comfortable means ever devised by man for carrying passengers in the air was the dirigible. These huge aerial ships, so painstakingly developed by the Germans during and after World War I, reached a degree of perfection with the *Graf Zeppelin* and the *Hindenburg,* both of which carried passengers on scheduled trans-Atlantic service during the mid-Nineteen-Thirties. In spite of the fact that one-way fares ran as high as $2250.00 for some of the first flights, later reduced to as little as $400.00, a dearth of customers seldom existed. Flying the ocean in the Thirties held attractions difficult to resist.

For one, the dirigible provided the means for crossing in a third of an ocean liner's time in a degree of almost equal elegance. For another, the trip offered a certain aura of daring at a time when trans-ocean aerial travel was virtually unknown by any other means.

The *Graf* first flew on September 18, 1928 and from then until 1937 made scheduled and non-scheduled passenger carrying trips throughout the world. By November 1935 it completed its 100th Atlantic crossing and carried 10,400 passengers. In 1936 it commenced regular flights to South America, a shuttle service which continued until May 7, 1937 —a fateful day in lighter-than-air history.

Her successful operations encouraged the construction of the bigger and far more powerful *Hindenburg* which began trans-Atlantic service between Friedrichshafen and Lakehurst on a clockwork schedule in 1936. While the *Graf* shuttled almost monotonously between Friedrichshafen and Rio de Janeiro, four days each way, the *Hindenburg* spanned the North Atlantic weekly. With the approach of winter, it joined the *Graf* in the South Atlantic, flying to Rio four times before the two retired for the season.

During its first year it had carried 3530 passengers and 66,000 pounds of cargo and mail at an average speed of 80 miles per hour, flying the West bound trip to Lakehurst in an average of 63 hours; 51 on the reverse leg.

Whereas the *Graf* carried its 20 passengers in the main gondola tucked up under the forward section of the hull, the *Hindenburg* provided quarters inside the ship itself, much like a bee-hive in a huge hollow tree. Here on two decks were spread out the accommodations for 50 passengers (later increased to 72)— staterooms decorated in the most modern manner, a half dozen toilets, shower, lounge (complete with 112 pound piano), dining room (measuring 16 feet by 46 feet and large enough to accommodate a full passenger list), galley, bar and smoking room. And in addition, running along either side of the passenger area, two long promenade decks from which the ground could be observed through a series of windows cut in the ship's outer skin.

In the galley, chefs cooked full course meals served in ocean liner fashion, on tables complete with linen cloths, silverware and china. For dirigible passengers were not confined to their seats and required to eat pre-cooked meals off trays sick-room style as on present day airliners. The trans-Atlantic passenger in 1936 lived graciously, eating, sleeping and relaxing in a most sumptuous manner, with complete freedom of movement throughout the passenger areas. And as though this were not enough to ask, on occasions he was allowed official inspections of the huge ship itself with visits to its bridge and examinations of its cavernous interior laced with girders, wires and ladders that led up to the monster's back, where crewmen oftentimes spent their leisure time sunbathing.

Only on rare occasions did the motion of either the *Graf* or the *Hindenburg* become noticeable, and rarely was it uncomfortable. For dirigibles, due to their immensity, flew through turbulence as calmly as a Rolls Royce travelling a corduroy road. Flying generally at altitudes less than 2000 feet and more often at half that amount and at a speed seldom exceeding

PASSENGERS BOARD *GRAF ZEPPELIN* on one of its scheduled flights across Atlantic between 1928 and 1937. By 1935 great aerial ship had completed its 100th Atlantic crossing and had carried 10,400 passengers.

75 MPH, dirigibles provided their passengers with unparalleled views of the terrain beneath. And with their relatively low-powered engines, mounted hundreds of feet behind the cabins, near silence enveloped their quarters. Vibration did not exist. A coin, set on edge on a table, would remain that way indefinitely during flight.

Vastness has always been a characteristic of airships and balloons, their physical size being grotesquely out of proportion with their carrying capacity. The *Graf,* for instance, 776′ long, weighing 258,000 pounds fully loaded, could carry but 20 passengers. The *Hindenburg,* 808′ long, 135′ in diameter with an all-up weight of 485,000 pounds, accommodated only 72. Their great advantage, of course, lay in their ability to cruise seven and eight thousand miles without refueling.

This unfavorable ratio of size to pay load is a characteristic of lighter-than-air craft, for helium and hydrogen—the only two gasses used—can lift just so much: an average of 74 pounds per thousand cubic feet for hydrogen; 69 for helium. It being impossible to modify the properties of these gasses, designers had but one recourse—build the vehicle large enough to contain the gas needed to lift the desired weight. The result was invariably cumbersome.

On May 7, 1937 the *Hindenburg* exploded over Lakehurst. The *Graf,* approaching Friedrichshafen at the time, completed her voyage, and from that moment on, never flew again. Along with a new *Graf Zeppelin* then undergoing her builder's trials over Germany, she was scrapped by order of Der Fuhrer.

Perhaps it was best that the end came as suddenly as it did for the dirigible otherwise might well have suffered a lingering death. Big and slow, expensive to build and maintain, requiring scores of ground crew men and elaborate equipment, it could not long compete with the airplane at the time rapidly approaching maturity.

GRAF ZEPPELIN **MOORS IN LOS ANGELES** following non-stop flight from Tokyo. Carrying 20 paying passengers, *Graf* completed 6,800 mile flight in 75 hours.

GRAF ZEPPELIN **STATEROOMS (below left)** and at right, passenger lounge on her first trans-Atlantic voyage.

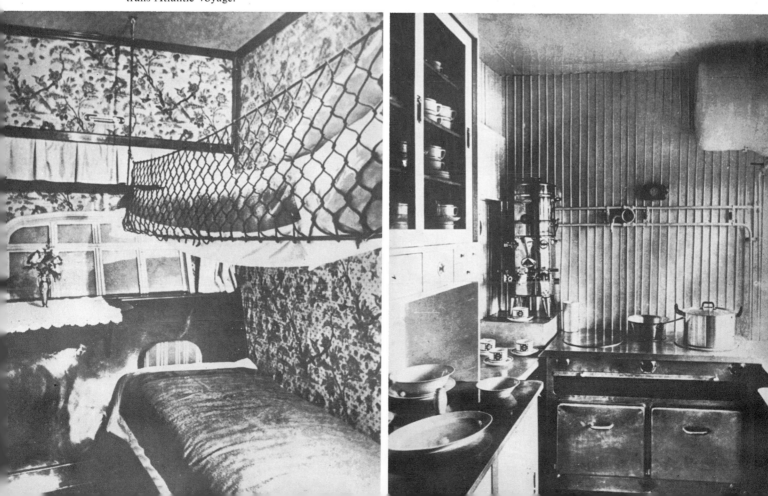

THE TWENTY PASSENGERS in the main gondola of *Graf Zeppelin* lived graciously with complete freedom of movement, eating and sleeping in luxury. Motion of ship was rarely noticeable.

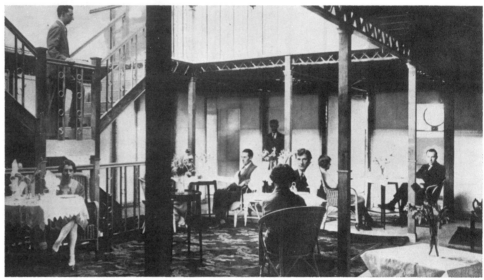

PASSENGER ACCOMMODATIONS on Britain's mighty dirigible *R-100*—1930. (Ship is shown next page.) Although it completed one round trip to Canada, *R-100* never proved successful. After loss of sister ship *R-101* on its maiden voyage, it was abandoned, along with Britain's entire lighter-than-air program.

DINING ROOM CORNER — Graf Zeppelin.

THOUSANDS FLOCKED TO ST. HUBERT AIRPORT in Canada to view Britain's giant *R-100*, which in 1931 had just completed trans-Atlantic crossing. Elaborate mooring mast at Montreal contained elevator which whisked passengers and crew to top, where they entered huge ship through nose hatch, then walked lengthy catwalk through interior of ship to their respective quarters amidship.

AERIAL RESTAURANT (left). Dining comfort aloft shown in Hindenburg's dining room. Never before had aerial passengers enjoyed meals in such comfort and quiet, never since has there been anything to equal it. Note promenade area in left part of photo with slanting windows looking out and down. Below is Hindenburg galley which served meals to all 72 passengers three times a day on trans-Atlantic crossings in 1937.

171

LANDING OPERATION. Mighty *Hindenburg* approaches field at Lakehurst, N.J. Ground crews have caught bow lines and are preparing to walk ship toward field's mooring mast.

NEW CONCEPT IN AIR TRAVEL. Boeing *707-120* — America's first commercial all-jet transport plane. Used by many of country's airlines, 248,000 pound machine can carry 121 to 179 passengers at 600 miles per hour for 4,000 miles. Such performance has changed concept of air travel as drastically as *DC-3* changed it in 1935.

V-DAY SENDS MODERN WINGS ALOFT

By the end of the war the pent up demand for civilian air transport burst its traces and in the United States alone, 12,591,251 people were carried—an increase of 2500 per cent in 20 years. The entire aircraft industry grew up almost over night, emerging mature, highly skilled and capable of completely revolutionizing aerial travel, which it immediately proceeded to do.

Because American manufacturers had been building passenger-carrying planes during the war years while other countries concentrated on military types, this country naturally had a corner on the commercial transport field when hostilities ceased. From 1946 to 1953 ninety percent of the world's commercial planes were American-built. Today, the old *DC-3*s still hold their own on short haul routes throughout the globe, giving no evidence of ever outwearing their usefulness. Douglas *DC-4*s, 6s and 7s continue in scheduled and non-scheduled use on the majority of long haul airlines this side of the Iron Curtain, along with Lockheed *Constellations,* Boeing *Stratocruisers, Convairs* and *Martins.*

Britain's efficient *Viscount* series has made an important place for itself in practically every major airline stable. Its pure jet *Comet* holds tremendous promise, and France's tail-jet *Caravel,* now built under license by Douglas, offers much for short and medium haul work. But United States' planes still predominate along the earth's far flung airways with its superb new jets rolling off production lines to nearly every operator in the world: the Boeing *707* jets, developed from the Air Force's *B-47* bomber, the Douglas *DC-8,* the Convair *880.*

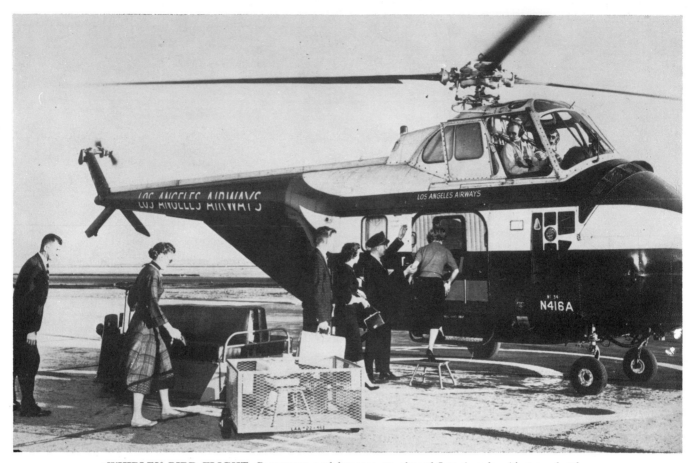

WHIRLEY BIRD FLIGHT. Passengers and baggage go aboard Los Angeles Airways shuttle helicopter en route to Santa Ana.

PASSENGERS TRANS-PORTED BY SNOW AUTO-VEHICLE to one of Iceland-air's *DC-3s* at airfield in Northern Iceland. This is typical present day usage of versatile old *DC-3*.

WORLD'S LARGEST PISTON-ENGINED TRANSPORT. Boeing *B-377 Stratocruiser*, as flying here for Northwest Orient Airlines, has won passenger acclaim as most luxurious commercial air liner ever built. In addition to main cabin and "luxury compartment" it has downstairs lounge seating 14. First introduced in 1946, is now being superseded by faster, more efficient jets and prop jets appearing in 1959.

ROUND TRIP TO CLEVELAND. Passengers at Pittsburgh ticket office of Pennsylvania Air Lines Inc. in 1931. Standing next to uniformed dispatcher is V. P. Clifford Ball who started line in April, 1927.

VISITORS FROM MARS? Before advent of pressurization oxygen masks were standard equipment aboard many airplanes. High altitude? Presto! Out came oxygen bottle. Here planeload of passengers aboard Northwest Orient Airlines Lockheed *14-H* enjoy trip over Rocky Mountains in mid-Thirties.

"CARE FOR BEEF TEA?" Interior British European Airways *Viking* in 1946 showing stewardess about to serve lunch.

IN FLIGHT AMUSEMENT on New Zealand National Airways airliner flying between Auckland and Fiji, July 1948.

"BRITISH EUROPEAN AIRWAYS FLIGHT 300 NOW LOADING." Passengers embarking on *Viscount 800* turbo-prop liner at London Airport Central.

FLEXIBLE TRANSPORTS. Until their retirement in August 1956, these four 72½ ton Martin JRM *Mars* seaplanes performed thrice-weekly airlifts between West Coast and Honolulu. Each remained in operation from six to eight months at a time. Minimums for safe operation in San Francisco Bay were lower than those for land plane flights at Oakland. *Mars* carried larger amounts of cargo, were more economical to operate than land-based competitor of same vintage.

HOW MANY—HOW HIGH—HOW FAR? Man's urge to see how many can be carried how high for how long goes on and on. In May 1949 Marshall *Mars* carried 301 passengers and 7 crew members from Alameda to San Diego, part of record load shown here.

BORN TWELVE YEARS TOO LATE. Three of these mighty *Princess* flying boats were built in England by Saunders-Roe in 1950 and 1951 for trans-ocean passenger carrying. They were largest seaplanes ever built, proved far too expensive to operate, no airline interested in using them. Minister of Supply agreed to cocoon them rather than break them up and this is undoubtedly how they will finish their days. They were never used for anything more than experimental work.

NOW IN NEVER-NEVER LAND. *Princess* boats were powered by ten Bristol *Proteus* turbine engines developing total 35,000 HP, turning counter-rotating props on four inboard units and single props on outboard. These engines gave speed of approximately 380 miles per hour and cruising radius of 5,500 miles, were designed to carry from 100 to 200 passengers, grossed 330,000 pounds.

CAPITAL VICKERS *VISCOUNT* **CIRCLES WASHINGTON (above left).** British-built airliners introduced by Capital Airlines were first turbo-props to enter commercial service in America. Center, passengers leave *DC-7* at Mexico City's modern airport in 1958.

DOOR-TO-DOOR DELIVERY. Los Angeles Airways helicopter delivering passengers direct to United Airlines flight.

INTER-AIRPORT HOP. New York Airways *44-B* helicopter approaching Heliport at foot of West 30th Street, Manhattan. 15 passenger choppers shuttle between New York Port Authority airports and this base on clocklike schedule, making circuit between LaGuardia, International, Newark and Heliport in just under 50 minutes. Typical fare—30th Street to LaGuardia—$5, time 9 minutes.

The helicopter came into its own during Korean War, has been used since with increasing intensity, proving to be ideal vehicle on inter-city feeder runs in big cities.

JET OVER HERTFORDSHIRE. De Haviland *Comet 4*, first jet liner to fly paying passengers on round trip trans-Atlantic flight—October, 1959. This 60 to 76 passenger plane, because of "buried" engines, presents sleekest appearance in commercial jet field.

HERCULES **BECOMES** *ELECTRA*. Eastern Airlines' version of Lockheed *Electra* which was developed from war carrier *C-130 Hercules*.

MODERN FLIGHT

TAKEOFF AT BRUSSELS. SABENA Sikorsky *S-38* hops up at Brussels airport.

5000 MILES AT 350 MILES PER HOUR. Pan American World Airways *DC-7C Clipper* represents ultimate development in piston-powered transoceanic aircraft. Total of 13,000 HP gives it cruising speed of 350 miles per hour which can be maintained for 5000 miles making non-stop Atlantic crossing commonplace. Seats from 69 to 99. Production of *DC-6s* and *DC-7s* phased out in 1958 after total of 1041 of all models had been constructed.

LAST WORD — AT PRESS TIME. Douglas *DC-8*.

All of this astonishing development of heavier-than-air craft has occurred during the last 55 years, starting slowly, building momentum slowly, but picking up in a geometric progression-like burst that has all but shoved man into outer space. His old urge to carry the most the highest and fastest continues to rage unabated.

APPENDIX I

THE STORY OF THE
SCHNEIDER TROPHY RACE

By HENRY R. PALMER, Jr.

ON the morning of April 6, 1913, four French hydroplanes—a Moraine Saulnier, a pair of Nieuports and a big black Deperdussin—all that could qualify of the 24 participating at Monaco that year, taxied fitfully around the harbor awaiting their turns to take off on the first Schneider Trophy Race.

To the winner three times within a five year period would go permanent possession of a silver trophy, a meager inducement, it would seem, to attract much serious competition, and yet here were four of the world's top speed pilots—three Frenchmen and one American—ready to battle it out. And in the years to come, nations would spend millions in the development of planes, and many a pilot would lose his life in an effort to win the contest—the greatest speed classic of the era.

Sponsored by French aviation enthusiast Jacques Schneider and designed primarily to promote interest in seaplane development, the contest mushroomed into an international free-for-all—a bitter contest between nations to produce the fastest conceivable racing planes, a series that did not end until Great Britain clinched her third race in September, 1931.

No other race ever did so much to create high speed aircraft in Europe and America, and in England's case, the knowledge and experience gained in producing planes for seven contests contributed immeasurably toward her victories in the Battle of Britain, for the sleek Supermarine monoplanes with which she whipped her competition in 1927, 1929 and 1931 sired the Spitfire—the deadly fighter that knocked so many Lufwaffe planes from her skies during her darkest hour.

Unlike all other great airplane races in which

Schneider Contestant at Olympia (England) Show. One of two Nieuports used in the 1913 Race. Reports and photos indicate the Nieuports planed better than their competitors, taking off in a more level attitude, thanks to their novel step design. The steps can barely be seen on the left float in the above photo. It is obvious they exist, however, for the edges of the bottoms (the chines) are raised some four or five inches from the floor. These floats were designed by a Lt. Delage of the French Navy and were built of cypress.
—Flight Photograph

pilots battled each other for the lead, crowding each other at the turns, bulling their way through the pack like racing cars, the Schneider races were run entirely against time.

To the thrill seeker this might well seem to be a mild way to run a race, scarcely worth the time and trouble to watch. But for the hoards who flocked to witness them over the years, they were the thrill supreme, for the purpose of the contest was to produce the fastest speed possible (unless a winner bettered the former mark by at least five miles per hour it was not recognized as a record) and to do this a pilot's attention could not be distracted by a sky full of screaming, angry rival planes. His job was to get the most out of his machine and its engine, an exacting job requiring exquisite skill and iron nerve. A sloppy turn or a brief climb could rob miles from his speed. Improperly

flown, the fastest plane could easily lose to a slower one in the hands of a masterful pilot.

Once all planes became airborne and in the circuit, however, it made little or no difference whether they were engaged in racing each other or not, for all were flying in the same direction, all were going full out, all were at the same low altitude. For the spectators, the thrill of such racing lay in the comparison of lap speeds, timed meticulously and announced on huge score boards at the early events and by loud speakers at the later ones.

Under the rules set up by the original Schneider committee, contestants were required to pass qualification tests a day before the actual race. Designed to weed out freak planes built solely for racing, the regulations called for each plane to taxi across the starting line (preferably in rough water) take off and land and then taxi at no less than 12 miles per hour for a half mile between a pair of buoys, repeat the process, and finally take off and land once more, crossing the line on the water. Thereafter, the plane was required to remain at anchor for six hours to prove its ability to float and otherwise behave correctly while moored.

All races were flown around a triangular or rectangular course (the choice lay with the contestants) at least 186 miles in length, and all of it over open water. A pilot could not accept outside help once the race had begun, although permitted to land anytime during it for repairs —providing he made them himself and with tools and spare parts carried on board. Planes could land to refuel, but only from their own supply. Other than these stipulations, there were no restrictions, and pilots were free to fly the course in any manner they chose so long as they crossed the starting line on the water, and rounded all the pylons.

All four planes used this April day were land planes converted to water use by the substitution of floats for wheels—a trend followed by practically every entry throughout the series. Prevost's Deperdussin, a mid-wing monoplane with a revolutionary shell-like fuselage (the monocoque form used in later years on American Lockheeds) straddled a pair of flat-bottom Tellier floats 13 feet long and 3½ feet wide. A small pontoon mounted at the rear prevented the tail assembly from sinking, for the center

of gravity was far back in this plane, a feature designed to angle it upward for easier takeoff. The weight could easily be counterbalanced by placing a man on the bow of each float.

The contestants had drawn lots to see who would start first, and Prevost had won. As the starting bomb exploded high overhead, he aimed for the starting line a good half mile away. In spite of its big 160 horsepower engine, his Deperdussin gained speed slowly, its blunt-bowed floats bulling their way through the choppy sea, tossing green water before them. A cloud of spray streamed out behind as the propeller picked it up and blew it back.

Gradually the floats reached the surface and the Dep was off, climbing slowly on the first leg of the rectangular course. For 28 laps it raced around the course, the exhaust from its clipped stacks snapping like a massive string of firecrackers, and crossed the finish line 2 hours and 50 minutes later. Judged the winner at a speed of slightly over 60 miles per hour, Prevost returned to shore only to be recalled a half hour later by a confused jury demanding that he cross the finish line again. Upon completion of this delayed ending, 58 minutes was added to his time, lowering his average to a mere 48 miles per hour.

Meanwhile, Roland Garros on an 80 horsepower Moraine, a splendid performer during the preceding days of the Monaco meet, failed for some unexplained reason to get off the

Savoia Marchetti S-19. The only plane to go the route in 1920.

Macchi 7. Italy's 1921 winner.

water. Espanet, flying the 100 horsepower Nieuport, dropped out after 45 miles with engine trouble, and American Charles Weyman, Gordon Bennett race winner in 1911, followed suit on his Nieuport.

So the victory went to Marcel Prevost, ironically the first and last Frenchman ever to win this French-sponsored affair.

1914

ENCOURAGED by Prevost's success the year before, eight French pilots entered the 1914 elimination contest (again held in Monaco), Prevost himself among them with another Deperdussin, this one powered with the new 200 horsepower 18 cylinder Gnome rotary engine. Roland Garros, who had recently flown the Mediterranean, appeared with a 160 horsepower Moraine Saulnier—twice as powerful as the one he had flown the previous year, while Espanet entered a 160 horsepower Nieuport. In addition to this formidable trio were two 160 horsepower Nieuports, a 160 horsepower Dep, a 100 horsepower Moraine-Saulnier and a Breguet biplane.

Of the eight, only three qualified, the rest falling by the wayside from a variety of engine disorders. Favorite Prevost withdrew early in the trials when the complex Gnome refused to produce sufficient power for takeoff, leaving only veterans Garros and Espanet and newcomer Levasseur to defend France's championship.

Both American entrants qualified easily, Weyman on a 160 horsepower Nieuport, and Thaw flying an ancient, rickety Curtiss pusher flying boat powered by a 100 horsepower Curtiss engine—a hopelessly outclassed machine, although apparently more dependable than five of the French planes.

Switzerland's lone entry (a 100 horsepower *FBA* flying boat), a British-built Deperdussin and a tiny Sopwith *Tabloid* biplane all passed the elimination trials and completed the complement of racers.

With the exception of the antiquated Curtiss boat and the Swiss *FBA*, the *Tabloid* looked less like a winner than any plane at the meet. A biplane, driven by a mere hundred horsepower, it sat clumsily on its boxy floats, its tail barely kept afloat by an aft pontoon, its elevators drooping in the water. And yet in the big race on the 20th it pulled a magnificent upset, winning it with ease with pilot Howard Pixton racking it around the turns in 60 and 70 degree banks the like of which Monaco had never seen before. Less than two weeks previously the little ship had turned turtle and sunk on its maiden flight in England when the big single float with which it had been equipped tripped on takeoff. Undaunted engineers quickly sawed the float in two, and mounted on the two halves, it handled without difficulty.

The ruling this year called for a pair of touch and go landings somewhere along the course during the race, and Pixton made his on the first lap. So nicely did this master pilot judge them that the difference in time between the first and second laps was less than 12 seconds.

For 14 laps he paced the pack, but on the 15th his engine began to miss. With only eight of the nine cylinders firing, he continued the race, still in the lead and with no apparent loss of speed, crossing the finish line 2 hours and 13 minutes after starting for an average speed of 85 miles per hour.

Of the eight starters, only Pixton and Burri in the *FBA* finished. Lord Carberry, England's second entry flying the Dep, failed to get back in the air after his first touchdown. The rear bank of cylinders on Espanet's Gnome heated up so badly he dropped out after 17 laps. Levasseur experienced the same trouble after 18. Burri landed for fuel after 20 laps and took off again, completing the race in 3 hours and 23 minutes.

1919

THE planes that assembled for the third Schneider race held at Bournemouth, England, in honor of Great Britain's victory in 1913, were a far more powerful and speedy lot than any that had appeared at the two previous meetings. Four years of war-driven need for aircraft had advanced the art of aeronautical engineering to a point undreamed of in 1913 and 1914, the airplane emerging remarkably advanced and grown up.

Engines on the seven entries ranged from 250 to 450 horsepower with potential speeds approaching 150 miles per hour—a far cry from Pixton's 85-mile-an-hour pace—but still a long way from what such tremendous horsepower should have produced. The art of streamlining was not yet fully understood.

Great Britain entered a 450 horsepower Sopwith seaplane, a Fairey seaplane and a Supermarine flying boat, each with the same power. France sent a pair of Nieuports with 300 horsepower Hispano-Suiza engines, and a 300 horsepower Spad biplane. Italy placed its hopes on a lone Savoia flying boat driven by a 250 horsepower Isotta-Fraschini engine—a clumsy looking machine compared with the others, but as it turned out, the only one to go the distance.

It was September 10th and all day the sea had been glassy smooth, while a thick haze had obscured the horizon and nearby reference points, making takeoffs and landings exceedingly dangerous. To make matters worse, the surface swarmed with debris neatly camouflaged by the inky water—a constant threat to paper-thin pontoons and hulls.

Conditions could hardly have been worse for such an important occurrence, and within minutes of the start all three French planes had sprung leaks from debris and hard landings, and retired. The British Supermarine crashed on takeoff, and the Fairey and Sopwith, unable to see the course markers ahead, aborted almost immediately after leaving the water.

The Savoia boat alone survived the ordeal, flying 10 laps at an average speed of 124.5 miles per hour, only to be disqualified immediately upon landing for having missed one of the

Macchi 19. 1921 entry.

Supermarine Sea Lion: Britain's 1922 Schneider winner.

markers each time around. Despite vehement Italian protests, the judges ruled no race, but as a consolatory gesture offered Italy the trophy to hold for a year and the right to stage the next race in her waters—a pair of offers she accepted with pleasure.

1920

IN spite of her poor luck at Bournemouth, Italy returned to the fray in 1920 undiscouraged and out to win. And her chances had never been better; for England (uncertain the prestige of winning matched the effort and cost) did not enter. Germany was down and out. The United States showed no interest, and at the last moment France withdrew her lone entry. This left the field clear for Italy, and in an uninspiring display, Captain Luigi Bologna went through the formalities of flying his 500 horsepower Savoia *S-19* boat around the 200 mile course at a lethargic 107 miles per hour—far less than the unofficial 1919 speed, but sufficient to clinch victory number one for Italy.

1921

IN the summer of 1921, "Aerial Age" commented editorially that the Schneider Cup Races had "degenerated into a one man show in which no one takes any particular interest." No one, that was, except Italy, the unofficial and official

winner of the two previous events, now fired by a burning determination to cop the series.

As host for 1921 she issued invitations for a race to be held at Venice on September 7. Only France accepted, entering a Nieuport-Delage twin float biplane powered by a 300 horsepower Hispano-Suiza engine. Italy, believing in safety in numbers, entered 10—the most any country ever produced for a single race.

By race day seven planes had been eliminated, and her fortunes rode on the remaining three: a Macchi 7 biplane flying boat powered by a pusher Isotta-Fraschini developing 200 horsepower, an exceedingly graceful Macchi *19* biplane boat with a 720 horsepower V-12 Fiat driving a 4-bladed tractor propeller, and a standard 250 horsepower Naval flying boat.

Two days before the race, the Nieuport-Delage cracked up and for the second time in two years Italy found herself minus any competition. She won the race in a remarkably lackluster manner, but it was well three planes had been chosen, for only one completed the relatively simple 200 mile flight. Zanetti's Macchi *19* caught fire, while Corrieglio on the Naval boat ran out of gas half way through the course. Briganti on the little Macchi 7 flew all ten laps, but at a mere 117 miles per hour—enough for an official win, but still short of the 1919 speed.

"Aerial Age" had certainly hit the nail on the head.

1922

WITH no other country showing the slightest interest in the forthcoming meet (this year to be held at Naples), Italy counted heavily on taking the silver prize for keeps. It seemed a safe bet the 1922 race would be another "one man show," but she had not reckoned on the spirit and enterprise of a British citizen who for two years had rankled at the Air Ministry's failure to uphold Britain's place in the air.

Hubert Scott-Paine, part owner and general manager of Supermarine Aviation Works, Ltd., that year took matters into his own hands, designing and building and paying for a special flying boat calculated to give the Italians a real run for their money.

Little about *Sea Lion's* appearance resembled a racing plane judged by later day standards (a conventional pusher biplane mounted on a massive vee-bottomed hull) and nothing particular distinguished it from Britain's 1919 Schneider entry except a far more powerful engine and a generally cleaned up exterior. But on race day it showed its tail feathers to Italy's best, never once relinquishing its lead, and flying the first six laps at 160 miles per hour—a phenomenal speed for such a clumsy boat and far faster than any Schneider racer had ever moved before.

At the end of lap six its pilot, Captain Biard, throttled back his 450 horsepower Napier to conserve it, loafing through the remaining rounds to win at an average speed of 145 miles per hour.

The Italians, amazed, disappointed and outclassed at what they had rightfully come to consider their own game, finished far behind, second place falling to a 300 horsepower Savoia *51*. With the race went their hopes for a clean sweep, and with England once again fired up, it appeared a foregone conclusion that competition in the future would not be limited entirely to Italian planes.

Navy-Curtiss CR3 flown to victory in 1923 Schneider Trophy Contest by Lt. David Rittenhouse (on pontoon).

Lt. James Doolittle stands on pontoon of his 1925 winning Curtiss R3C2, Baltimore, Md.

1923

TEN years after the first Schneider race had been staged, America entered the contest for the first time—and won it hands down.

Staged off England's Isle of Wight, the race also attracted teams from Britain and France, but Italy had withdrawn a week before the big day—September 28th—claiming a lack of time to complete its two new racers—a Savoia and a Macchi.

The United States Navy sent four twin float Curtiss biplanes and a team of hand picked pilots: Lieutenants Wead, Rittenhouse, Irvine and Gorton, the latter assigned to its most powerful ship, a 700 horsepower Navy-Wright that had been clocked at better than 180 miles per hour.

Two of the planes (Curtiss CR3s) had flown as land planes in the 1921 and 1922 Pulitzer Trophy races. Pulled out of retirement, equipped with pontoons and vitalized with new 465 horsepower Curtiss D-12 water cooled engines, they had made 194 miles per hour—a figure softened in pre-race publicity notices to something in the neighborhood of 175 miles per hour. The fourth plane, a TR3A, built by the Naval Aircraft

Factory along the lines of the 1922 winner of the Curtiss Marine Flying Trophy race, packed the least amount of punch—a Wright E4 developing but 265 horsepower.

Unfortunately, the hot NW-2 damaged its floats before race day and could not fly, a bitter disappointment to American supporters who had looked upon this speed demon as a sure winner. Its designers, conscious of the need to streamline, yet faced with the problem of how to fair the huge radiators required to cool such an immense power plant, installed them on both surfaces of the upper wing and the top surface of the lower—a method copied by other countries in the years to follow.

Great Britain entered the fray with the same Supermarine Sea Lion that had won for her in 1922. Two other entries, a 450 horsepower Sopwith Hawker and a 450 horsepower Blackburn flying boat (whose hull dated back to 1918) had crashed a few days before the contest.

The French team fared almost as badly. Starting off with a pair of CAMS flying boats powered by 360 horsepower Hispano-Suizas and two Latham boats driven by twin 400 horsepower Lorraine Dietrichs, it ended up with a single *CAMS*—crackups and engine problems eliminating the others.

Blessed with shining clear weather, the racers (seven all told) approached the starting line. At 11 o'clock sharp Lieut. Irvine on one of the *CR3s* took off and streaked for the first mark. Lieut. Rittenhouse on the second *CR3* followed immediately behind, but the *TR3* piloted by Wead developed engine disorders and couldn't make it.

As Irvine finished the first lap, Britain's *Sea Lion* took off. Three of the French planes followed, but only one made it. The Latham's tandem engines balked at the last moment, and one of the *CAMS* fouled a buoy. M. Hurel on the remaining *CAMS* took off, but on the second lap his engine began misfiring, bringing him back down again in a hurry.

From the start it became apparent the American planes would win, barring mechanical failures. Far faster than the old *Sea Lion* and much more maneuverable, they tore around the turns in the smoothest display of flying ever witnessed at a Schneider race.

Rittenhouse won, flying the 200 miles in 1 hour and 12 minutes at an average speed of 177 miles per hour. Irvine finished second at 173 miles per hour, while Biard on the *Sea Lion* placed third at 157 miles per hour.

If any one factor could be claimed for the Americans' success, it was their designer's attention to streamlining and fairing. No cleaner planes had ever been seen at the Schneider

races before, and their appearance and superior performance changed the conception of high speed flying throughout the world. From this point on speeds of racing planes would begin the remarkable climb that has continued to the present day.

1925

AMONG the airplanes participating in the 1925 contest held that year at Baltimore in honor of America's victory in 1923, was a Curtiss *R3C2 Racer* entered by the United States Army Air Services—the first and only Army plane to take part in the series. Piloted by the incomparable Lieut. Jimmy Doolittle, it rocketed around the course at 232 miles per hour, beating out its nearest competitor, a British Gloster, by 33 miles per hour.

A race had been scheduled at Baltimore the previous year, but the crash of Britain's main hope (a Gloster Napier) a few weeks before the October date, eliminated her from the race. Neither Italy nor France could make it, and the United States, unwilling to fly it without outside competition, postponed it to the next year —a fine sporting gesture greatly appreciated by the other countries, but never repeated by them on similar occasions in future years.

Of the other seven planes participating that year, only three finished the 218 mile course: an Italian Macchi flying boat, the Gloster and Doolittle's *R3C2*. The others fell by the wayside from a variety of ills common to such high

Macchi 39, deBernardi's winner at 246 MPH, 1926.

Macchi 52. One of Italy's 1927 entries.

strung racing machines. A spin from a hundred feet wrecked Britain's chief hope, a sleek Supermarine monoplane—first of its kind to be used in the Schneider—a plane that had made 226 miles per hour in practice flights. Rough water nearly swamped her second entry, a Napier powered Gloster. The engine of one of Italy's Macchis balked at the start and the ship was abandoned. An American Curtiss *R3* flown by Lieut. Cuddihy ran out of oil on the last lap and burst into flames in mid-air. On the sixth lap, the Navy's other hope, Lieut. Ofstie's Curtiss Racer, dropped out with engine trouble.

The day was perfect for seaplane racing: bright sun, light chop and a 15 mile wind. On the dot at 2:35 Doolittle taxied toward the starting line, crossing it full out two minutes later. Flying low and rounding the pylons in faultless vertical banks he made the first circuit at 223 miles per hour to the amazement and delight of the large crowd of spectators lining the shore areas that bordered the route. At the end of lap two, the speed had increased to 233 and there it hovered throughout the 56 minutes it took him to complete the course.

Never before had any Schneider racer flown so fast, and never had a pilot handled his plane with such consummate skill, completely outclassing Britain's Captain Broad in the Gloster Napier and deBriganti in the Macchi. Broad finished at an average speed of 199 miles per hour—faster than the *Sea Lion's* winning time in 1923—while deBriganti placed third at 168 miles per hour. Considering the fact the Italian

was flying an out-and-out flying boat (an awkward looking monoplane whose wing cleared the water by less than two feet) his speed was remarkably good. But it became perfectly apparent from that moment on that flying boats could no longer be expected to win races. Their speed potentials had long since passed.

1926

HAVING won the 1921 and 1922 races, Italy now determined to cop the 1926 event to keep alive its chances for permanent possession. Accordingly she sent to America a trio of superb low wing monoplanes—blood red Macchi 39s—all identical, all powered by 800 horsepower 12 cylinder Fiat engines, and all manned by highly trained crews.

Britain and France failed to enter the contest, but America dragged out her old standbys—the three Curtiss racers used in previous events, including Doolittle's ancient *R3C2*. Two were repowered: the *R3C4* with a 700 horsepower Curtiss D-12, and the *R3C3* with a geared down 700 horsepower Packard V-1500. No engine changes were made in Doolittle's *R3C2*, and the only other major modifications to any of the planes was the installation of newly-designed floats and Reed all-metal propellers.

The United States, more concerned with pilot safety perhaps, and much more conservative pricewise than the other countries, had stuck with this basic fighter design created in 1921—

Supermarine S-5 (left) and Gloster-Napier, two of Britain's entries in 1927 race sit on dollies at Venice.

a fast, highly maneuverable ship stressed for the most violent acrobatics and possessing the remarkably high safety factor of twelve. As a land plane Doolittle's ship had won the Pulitzer race in 1925 at an average speed of 248 miles per hour over a 124 mile course for a world record, and the day after winning the Schneider that year, he flew it to a 245 mile an hour seaplane record.

They were slow to reach planing speed, however, their highly loaded, razor sharp wings lifting little or nothing under 50 miles per hour. Every ounce of power their engines could exert was needed to pull the big floats up to the surface and over the "hump," a trick requiring great pilot skill, for control surfaces were small and ineffective at low speeds.

The controllable pitch propeller had not been perfected, and designers faced the problem of creating a propeller that could produce maximum speed in the air while retaining sufficient thrust for takeoff. Getting airborne could be as difficult as starting an Indianapolis racing car up hill in high gear.

Propeller torque proved a tremendous hazard, especially on the geared down *R3C3* whose right float submerged completely at full throttle. In this dangerous position it wallowed helplessly, tossing water into the prop, its wing tip dragging, its controls ineffective. Use of opposite rudder to counteract torque merely created more drag, and Lieut. Tomlinson soon learned there was nothing he could do under these conditions but ignore the controls and let the plane work

out of its dilemma alone. Once on the step, free from the clutching water, it accelerated rapidly, porpoising and tossing clouds of spray but getting into the air like a shot.

Unfortunately, the gearing of the *R3C3's* propeller spun it to the right requiring the use of *left* rudder to counteract its torque. For pilots used to right rudder this reversal proved disconcerting, and may have been a factor in the crack up of the plane a few hours before the race.

Race day sparkled. A light chop kicked up by a northwest breeze provided a perfect takeoff surface. An hour before starting time, the pilots fired up their engines, warming them slowly on shore, mechanics hovering around them listening for the slightest sounds of trouble.

One by one they rolled off their ramps on their dollies into the water, each one surrounded by handling crews in bathing suits and waders, working in water up to their middles, pulling the beaching gear clear of the pontoons. Afloat, the pilots gunned their engines, hurling back clouds of spray on the already drenched crew men, and headed for the general starting area.

The roar that poured from the clipped exhaust stacks mixed with the blat of the props as they bit into the spray and created a din that could be heard for miles, a long, high pitched howl that sent shivers of delight through the crowds lining the shore.

Lt. Bacula took off first, his Macchi leaving the water smoothly after a 25 to 30 second run and made a bee line for the first marker, nine and a half miles out in Chesapeake Bay. Tomlinson crossed the line as Bacula sped by on the far horizon on the second leg. Cuddihy in the *R3C4* started as Bacula completed lap one—at a slow 209 miles per hour—a pace he would maintain throughout the race to conserve his engine, thereby assuring Italy of a place should either of the two Macchis fail.

A minute after Cuddihy's takeoff, Captain Ferrarin shot across the line. Minutes later Cuddihy crossed the line and a shout went up from the crowd at the announced speed—232 miles per hour.

At that point Captain deBernardi crossed the line a minute ahead of Lieut. Schildt in Doolittle's *R3C2*, and now all six planes were in the circuit together, streaking around it at varying speeds and at altitudes less than 200 feet.

The Italian planes, blowing black smoke from their exhausts, their engines screaming, cut the pylons wide, while the Americans in their more maneuverable ships banked vertically around them.

At the end of lap three Ferrarin force landed with a broken oil line. Cuddihy dropped out at the end of the sixth, the victim of a bad fuel pump. But the other four finished, deBernardi winning at a speed of 246 miles per hour. Schildt in the *R3C2* averaged 230 miles per hour for

second place, Bacula placed third at 214, while Tomlinson in the *Hawk* came in last at a measly 137 miles per hour.

It had been a good race—one of the best—with Italy winning it fairly and squarely with the cleanest, most powerful planes the Schneider series had ever seen. But the entire concept of the contest had changed, for Jacques Schneider's original wish to promote interest in seaplaning had degenerated into a madcap struggle for speed supremacy using planes built only for racing and good for nothing else.

Italy, however, had accomplished exactly what she had set out to do. Her chances now for permanent possession of the prized trophy had never looked better.

1927

WITH two victories and a pair of near misses under her belt and a chance to keep in the running with a win in 1927, America chose to drop out of the contest entirely, aparently oblivious to the advantages of high speed plane development.

Unofficially she might have been represented by a single entry, a superb 1200 horsepower racing biplane sponsored by Packard and a

A Supermarine S-5, 1929 model, is wheeled out of its hangar.

group of New York business men, had its bugs been ironed out in time. But they weren't, and it was scratched at the last moment.

France failed to enter a plane, and the contest boiled down to a duel between England and Italy, each determined to win, each armed with the finest stable of thoroughbred racers money could buy and skill devise.

England sent seven planes—three new Supermarine S-5s, a pair of stubby little Gloster Napier biplanes, and a highly experimental air-cooled Short-Bristol monoplane known simply as the "Crusader."

Italy entered three Macchi 52s, somewhat smaller than the M-39s it had used the year before, but heavier and considerably more powerful. With their 1030 horsepower Fiats, their straightaway speeds approached 300 miles per hour.

Like race horses, these delicate, powerful, tremendously fast planes bred only for speed were useless for anything else. High strung and skittish, hard to fly and almost impossible to see out of dead ahead, they demanded (and got) the most concentrated attention from their pilots. Structurally they could withstand the normal forces of passing through turbulent air at maximum speeds but little more, and pilots were careful to avoid any undue stresses such as might be encountered rounding pylons at too steep an angle.

Britain's team of pilots this year, Kinkhead, Webster and Worsley, were unknown in racing circles, but all were ultra-hot service pilots picked for their ability to fly fast planes and to fit in the tiny cockpits, for this batch of planes showed the least frontal area of any racers before them—smaller floats, sharper wings and narrower fuselages that only a small man could shoehorn his way into.

Each man had been virtually ordered by the Air Ministry to bring the trophy back to Great Britain, for this was a do or die struggle. With America out, it remained only for England to beat Italy three times in a row to be crowned undisputed champion of the world—a title she badly wanted.

Italy's triumvirate—Major deBernardi, Captain Arturo Ferrarin, and Captain George Guazzetti—were a seasoned lot, fully capable of flying on even terms with the world's best aviators. Britain's team would have its hands full downing these experts.

Between the two teams existed an intense rivalry spurred on by their government's cravings for the prestige such an important victory would bring. This was to be no friendly meeting of seaplane enthusiasts. This would be a bitter effort to show the world who led in air power.

The course this year ran the length of the Lido, Venice's 15 mile stretch of beach on the Adriatic, a superior raceway in every respect, for its straight white line of sand guided the planes unerringly to the pylons placed at either end.

The Lido also proved nearly perfect for the spectators—those who were lucky enough to find transportation across the lagoon from Ven-

Supermarine S-6B, the 1931 winner at 340 MPH.

Macchi 72: Italy's 440 mile per hour, twin engine, counter rotating propeller racer.

ice—for it provided an unobstructed view of the planes as they hurtled along its length a few dozen feet above the surf.

Thousands of people had descended on Venice to witness this race, along with members of nobility and government: the Crown Prince and his entourage, Under Secretary of State for Air, His Excellency Italo Balbo with his staff of Royal Italian Air Force officers, General Francisco de Pinedo, and a multitude of lesser individuals. From England came Under Secretary for Air, Sir Phillip Sassoon and his staff of officers to witness the affair—one not looked upon lightly by air-conscious Europe.

The city had taken on a carnival-like air complete with bands, flags, posters. The Piazza San Marco swarmed with joyous holiday throngs, relaxed, arguing good naturedly on the merits of the various planes and speculating on their chances. Speeds of 280 miles per hour were freely predicted for the winner, and the odds leaned heavily toward that man being an Italian.

But the Italians were doomed to disappointment, for not one of their planes completed the race. Major deBernardi dropped out after the first lap with engine trouble. Ferrarin's engine failed moments after takeoff, and Captain Guazzetti's let him down just after completing the fifth.

England's Gloster-Napier, after streaking around the course five times at a sizzling 277 mile an hour speed, force landed after losing its propeller spinner. But the two S-5s performed flawlessly with Webster winning at a 281 mile an hour average, and Worsley following close behind at 271.

It had been a clear cut victory for England, and a triumph for Supermarine and Rolls-Royce. But it had been a crushing blow to Italy whose hopes had been so high.

1929

ON the afternoon of September 13th, 1929, a vast crowd estimated by some to contain upwards of a million people gathered in Southern England to witness what had loudly been advertised as the greatest aeronautical spectacle of all time—the 11th Schneider Cup Race.

The crowd swarmed along both shores of the Solent, that body of water separating England's rocky headlands from the Isle of Wight roughly five miles to the south, and packed itself aboard a huge armada of boats of every description ranging from punts and sailing wherries to steam yachts and ocean liners chartered specially for the occasion. A pair of England's

One of Great Britain's Supermarine S-6Bs, second place winner at Calshot, 1931. Note extreme length of floats, and oil cooler tubes running along fuselage.

—Underwood & Underwood

mightiest carriers, "Argus" and "Furious," their decks packed with military planes, and a handful of lesser naval vessels anchored nearby, lending a note of authority to the affair.

By mutual consent of the contestants, the 1928 race had been omitted, for by this time the cost of designing and building such complicated machines as Schneider racers had risen far too high for even the richest countries to bear every year. By skipping a year it was hoped all four major air powers could partake in 1929, and for a time it appeared all would attend, but by race day France had dropped out following the death of her ace pilot while testing one of her entries, and America's unofficial representative —Lieut. Al Williams—again failed to ready his special racer in time. The field lay open to Great Britain and Italy, both of whom appeared with a collection of the highest powered, fastest planes ever gathered for a Schneider race.

Italy entered three 1750 horsepower Macchi 67s, a tiny 1000 horsepower Fiat described by one reporter as "the most beautiful piece of work at Calshot," and a revolutionary Savoia-Marchetti monoplane powered by twin 1000 horsepower Isotta-Fraschini engines mounted in tandem, one in front of and one behind the pilot. The 1927 Macchi M-52 that had raced in

1927 and had broken the world speed record in 1928 tagged along as a standby. A second Macchi 67—one on which Italy had counted heavily—had crashed a few days before the race killing its pilot and all but ruining her chances of winning.

Britain's hopes rode on a pair of brand new 1900 horsepower Supermarine S-6s, a Gloster-Napier that had balked repeatedly during trials, and the 1927 S-5 brought along for a spare.

The S-6 was the most powerful Schneider racer to date, and it was also the most powerful single engined plane in the world. To absorb the tremendous thrust of its supercharged Rolls-Royce engine, its propeller had been geared down like the one on America's 1926 Curtiss racer and with exactly the same results: its torque buried the left float the instant full power was applied. Experiments with a larger float and hydrovanes merely aggravated the situation and caused the ship to porpoise so badly in attempts to take off that onlookers wondered what held it together.

Here indeed was need for a propeller whose pitch could be changed in flight, for all the S-6 needed was low pitch to get off and the ability to shift to high aloft. But no such device existed in 1929 forcing Supermarine to change to a finer pitch propeller. With this, the S-6 managed a successful but slow (45 second) takeoff.

By 1929 Schneider engines had grown so powerful that designers were hard pressed to devise methods of keeping them cool at full throttle. The flush-wing radiator, introduced by the Americans on the 1923 Curtiss plane and used on all participating planes in subsequent years, had worked well enough for the lower powered engines. But it was never wholly satisfactory for the larger engines, and proved completely inadequate for the 1900 horsepower Rolls-Royce in the S-6 which generated more heat than any engine built before.

To cool it, Supermarine engineers converted the entire wing into a radiator by enveloping it with a duraluminum water jacket through which flowed the nearly steaming water from the hot engine.

Lubricating oil, pumped piping hot at eight gallons a minute, passed through finned tubes on each side of the fuselage to a cooling tank in the vertical stabilizer, thence back to the engine. So critical did engine heat become on these less-than-hour-long races, that pilots flew entirely by the water temperature gauge holding them between 200 and 210 by skillful throttle jockeying.

No air cooled engine of the day approached the power of the Rolls-Royce and the Lyon, and even if one had existed it is probable its great frontal resistance would have proved too much drag for speeds in the 300 miles per hour class. Water cooled engines were easier to streamline and the forward ends of the planes they powered were characteristically sharp. With no radiators, with a beautifully faired engine cowl, with recessed exhaust ports and a fuselage so narrow its pilot could scarcely squeeze into it, the S-6 presented a minimum of head resistance. Only the bulky floats (and even they were more streamlined than conventional landing wheels) remained to create drag—a drag of immense proportions at 300 mile speeds.

The six planes sitting on their ramps on race day that year were a delicate lot, untried for the most part and untested. Britain's S-6 had accumulated less than two and a half hours flying time before the race. The ill-starred Gloster-Napier, a week before the race, had flown for less than a minute. Flying time of one of the Macchi 67s totaled but 15 minutes by race day, and the second M-67 had never been off the water.

The big day dawned sunny and warm, the surface of the water rippled perfectly for take-offs by a steady 10 knot breeze. Flight Leader Waghorn was first to start, roaring across the line at precisely 2 o'clock, and on his first lap broke the world's speed record by flying it at 324 miles per hour. Increasing his speed gradually on the following laps, Waghorn reached 331 at which point he throttled back a hundred revolutions to save fuel and to prevent his engine from boiling over.

Flight Leader Atcherley took off next and soon had the lap speed up to a furious 332 miles per hour flying his S-6 masterfully despite the loss of his goggles and therefore nearly blind. Dal Molin in one of the Macchi 52s left over from the 1927 race, started third, followed by Cadringher in a Macchi 67—Italy's latest and most powerful single engined racer. Approaching the first pylon at nearly 300 miles per hour and banked over at 20 degrees, Cadringher skidded badly, nearly stalled, recovered and eventually squared himself off on the next lap. But fumes from the middle set of cylinders on the big Fiat had been blowing back into his face since takeoff and, unable to see clearly, he abandoned the race before completing the second lap. Monti, on the second M-67, after making 301 miles per hour on lap one, dropped out with engine trouble at the beginning of the second. Flight Lieut. Greig, flying the old S-5, plugged along at a consistent 282 mile an hour pace, varying less than 2 miles per hour throughout the seven circuits.

Waghorn won it at an average clip of 328 miles an hour (indicating speeds probably hit 350 on the straightaways). Dal Molin placed second at 284 and Greig took third at 282.

The British pilots had developed a technique of starting their banks far out from the pylons, throttling down as they approached them to avoid blacking out, then whipping around them in a near vertical attitude. Once around, they straightened out rapidly, and opened their throttles wide.

The Italians, on the other hand, took the turns slower, skidding up and out, but recovering their lost speed by diving back once the mark had been rounded.

But whatever the technique, the fact remained clear for anyone to see: Great Britain was far out ahead in aircraft and engine design and Italy, with the full count on her, sat in a precarious spot.

1931

ON September 13, 1931, Great Britain's Lieut. J. N. Boothman won the Schneider Trophy for keeps by flying his 2300 horsepower Rolls-Royce Supermarine S-6 around the 217 mile course at Calshot at an average speed of 340 miles an hour with no competition save fellow pilot Lieut. G. H. Stainforth in a second S-6.

It had been a bad year for the other countries, and no one had turned up. Two of Italy's crack Schneider pilots, Monti and Bellini, had been killed that year testing racers, and all efforts to perfect her stupendous twin engine Macchi (a project that had been going on for two years) had failed miserably. Regretfully Italy backed out.

France also had lost an ace pilot shortly before race day and when it became apparent her two speedsters—a special Nieuport and a 1900 horsepower Bernard—could not be completed in time, she too withdrew. America again failed to enter a plane. England would have missed the race entirely following an Air Ministry decision to abandon it had it not been for the generosity and public spiritness of one Lady Houston who had donated $500,000.00 of her own money to finance the venture. England, too, had lost a pilot and one of her planes less than a month before the race. But now, ready, willing and able and challenged by the others, she saw no logical reason for postponing the event. If they were not ready it was through no fault of hers.

·There were those who criticised her for running the race alone. America had refused to do it in 1924. But Italy had done it in 1920 and

Torque from its mighty Rolls-Royce engine buries the left float of this Supermarine S-6 leaving its ramp for a practice flight. Lt. G. B. Brinton, R.N., pilot, Calshot, 1931.   —*Underwood & Underwood*

1921 and Italy now was England's main challenger. In her defense it must be said her planes flew the course at full speed, not loafing around the course as well they might have to conserve their engines. Her pilots could never have preferred to win it alone. There was little satisfaction in the one-sided victory, and for the crowds who had again poured out to witness the event, the ending was little more than a sickly sort of anti-climax.

And so the Schneider trophy at long last had found a permanent home. By winning five races (more than any other country) England deserved the honor. It was regrettable that Jacques Schneider's own country could manage no more than a single win—not even a place in the others—but such are the fortunes of racing.

There had been other International races before—the Rheims, the Gordon Bennett—but no series had lasted as long as the Schneider, and no other had produced such phenomenal speeds.

Individually, the races had never proved particularly exciting, for all had been run against time. Many had been badly flown. Some lacked the slightest semblance of competition. There had been no accidents, no close calls, nothing dramatic to thrill the crowds or to show up the risks involved in this sort of flying.

The Contest had not accomplished what Jacques Schneider intended it to accomplish, for it had not fostered the development of private seaplane flying, and had he lived to see the last race flown he might well have objected to the course the event had taken. But he never could have denied that it had done wonders for high speed flying, for during its 18-year span speeds climbed steadily from 60 miles an hour to 340, and had Italy's twin engine, 2000 horsepower Macchi performed on September 13th, 1931, as it should have and as it did three years later when it hit 440 miles an hour, the record would have been even more impressive.

From this point of view, the Schneider Contest had been eminently successful.

APPENDIX II

THE 1903 WRIGHT BIPLANE

Span: 40 feet 4 inches (The right wings were four inches longer than the left to provide additional lift for the engine which was placed to the right of center and which weighed 34 pounds more than the operator who lay to its left.)
Length: 21 feet 1 inch
Chord: 6 feet 6 inches
Gap: 6 feet 2 inches
Wing area: 510 square feet
Weight: 605 pounds (minus operator)
Power: 12 HP Wright 4-cylinder water cooled
Speed: Approximately 10 MPH into a 20-30 mile wind.

The Wrights had agreed that all flying would be done that December morning near the ground for the sake of personal safety, and consequently they held their altitude as close to ten feet as the gusty wind and their lack of flying skill permitted. The ground speed on these flights barely exceeded ten miles per hour—slow enough for a man to run beside it as it flew its wavy course down the beach.

Twin pusher propellers were used on this plane to double the amount of thrust against a greater surface of air, and to counteract gyroscopic action which the Wrights feared would result from use of a single propeller. The two ran in opposite directions, a feat accomplished by crossing the driving chains on the right hand side. As these ran through steel tubes, there was no danger that they might become entangled. So successful did this method of propulsion prove that it was used on all subsequent Wright planes with but one exception through 1915.

THE 1908 WRIGHT BIPLANE

Span: 41 feet
Chord: 6 feet 6 inches
Gap: 6 feet
Wing area: 512 square feet
Weight: (approximately) 800 pounds
Power: 30-40 HP Wright 4-cylinder water cooled.
Speed: (approximately) 34 MPH

A number of planes were built by the Wrights between 1907 and 1909 and dimensions varied. The above specifications are a close approximation of the model pictured.

THE BLERIOT *XI*

Span: 28 feet 6 inches
Wing area: 160 square feet
Weight: 650 to 720 pounds
Power: Various engines used, from a 3-cylinder Anzani developing 23 HP to the 50 and 100 HP Gnomes.
Speed: With Anzani, 36 MPH
With 50 HP Gnome, 48 MPH
Power loading: 14.4 pounds per HP
Wing loading: 4.5 pounds per square foot.

There were so many variations of the Bleriot XI series that the above specifications are only a close approximation.

BRISTOL *Boxkite*

Span: 33 feet
Length: 38 feet 6 inches
Height: 11 feet
Area: 457 feet
Weight loaded: 900 pounds
Speed: 40 MPH
Power: 50 HP Gnome
Power loading: 9 pounds per HP
Wing loading: 1.9 pound per foot.

THE 1909 FARMAN MACHINE

Span: 33 feet
Length: 33 feet 6 inches
Chord: 6 feet 6 inches
Gap: 7 feet
Wing area: 430 feet
Weight: 1100 pounds (minus pilot)
Speed: 37 MPH
Power: 7 cylinder 50 HP Gnome rotary engine, placed at the rear of the fuselage and driving an 8½ foot diameter propeller mounted in *front* of it.

This was a slow and clumsy machine, but dependable as early planes went, its low speed practically precluding damage to its occupants. Its extremely low wing-loading gave it great stability and load carrying characteristics second to none. Farmans were widely used in Europe for training and racing.

Vertical direction was controlled by a large lever on the pilot's right hand side. Forward and backward motion of this lever tilted the big elevator mounted in front of him on long outriggers. Sideways motion moved the wing flaps, or ailerons, which hung free at the end of each wing and drooped down when the plane was at rest. In flight they streamed out like flags, free to be pulled down individually when a turn was to be made. Twin rudders in the rear were operated by a pivoted foot bar.

Wing loading was 2.8 pounds per square foot of surface. Power loading was 24 pounds per HP.

1910 FARMAN

Span: 38 feet
Wing area: 429 feet
Chord: 6 feet 6 inches
Weight: 1200 pounds
Maximum capacity: 680 pounds
Speed: 37 MPH
Engine: Gnome 50 HP, 7 cyl.

The outstanding characteristics of the H. Farman were the drooping ailerons, the pusher prop attached *ahead* of the engine and the excessive gap between wings.

In the model illustrated herewith, ailerons were located only on the top wings, but on earlier Farmans they hung from both. They were not interconnected in the manner of present day ailerons, only one working at a time. Note slackness in cables attached to control stick in Farman's hand. See photo Page 36.

Apparently Farman felt better engine cooling and propeller efficiency would result from the unorthodox method of engine suspension, but he certainly showed little or no respect for the poor mechanic who had to spin it trapped as he was between outriggers.

Most planes of this era had extremely "soft" landing gears to absorb the shock of fast landings, which approached top speed. The Farman was no exception. Note arrangement whereby wheel axles were attached to long fore and aft skids with heavy shock cord. Excessively hard landings stretched the cords allowing skids to drag thereby effectively killing off excess speed.

CHAR-A-BANC

Span: 62 feet
Length: 37 feet 6 inches
Wing area: 790 square feet
Power: 120 HP 6 Cylinder water cooled Austro-Daimler
Average speed: 76 MPH
Fuel: 28 gallons
Capacity: 5 (Carried 10 on at least one occasion)

THE *AERO BUS* AND *AERO TAXI*

Span: 43 feet
Length: 46 feet
Wing area: 439 feet
Weight (bus): 1323 pounds
Weight (taxi): 1540 pounds
Power: 100 HP Gnome Rotary, 14 cylinder

THE 1910 CODY

Span: 46 feet
Length: 38 feet 6 inches
Wing area: 540 square feet
Useful load: 800 pounds
Speed: 38-52 MPH
Capacity: 2
Power: 60 HP Green (In 1912 with a 120 HP Austro-Daimler, this machine carried 5.)

THE 1912 CODY

Span: 43 feet 6 inches
Length: 38 feet 6 inches
Wing area: 260 square feet
Useful load: 750 pounds
Speed: 58-83 MPH
Capacity: 2
Power: 120 HP Austro-Daimler
Rate of Climb: 288 feet per minute
Ceiling: 6000 feet
Range: 336 miles

THE 1910 SOMMER BIPLANE

Span: 33 feet
Chord: 5 feet 2 inches
Wing area: 326 square feet
Weight: 800-900 pounds
Power loading: 16 pounds per HP
Wing loading: 2¾ pounds per square foot
Power: 50 HP Gnome
Speed: 46 MPH

This plane had been built in 1909 for Roger Sommer by Henri Farman and on it Sommer made a number of impressive records including one 109 mile flight in the 1910 Michelin race.

WALDEN III 1909-1910
The first all-American monoplane

(From specifications prepared by Dr. Henry M. Walden, Oct. 1956)

Anzani engine, 3 cylinder, 25 HP, air cooled. All controls on wheel excepting lateral balance. Automatic lateral balance was effected successfully by two ear-shaped fins, one above each extremity. These fins were hinged to a supporting bracket at about one third their length, and held to an anterior bracket by properly tensioned springs. In normal flight these fins were subject to negative pressures which held them at slight negative angle to the line of flight. In a lateral dip, they assumed a positive angle limited to a certain degree of inclination.

These fins were very effective, but prevented holding the plane to a bank and made turning efforts effective only in very wide circles, for which reason they were later discarded in the construction of the Walden VII and following models.

Landing and top speeds were not definitely determined. This plane cracked up on August 3, 1910 when the Anzani blew a cylinder at a height of about 100 feet.

Tires were of the motorcycle type. Wing covering was doped Irish linen.

THE HANRIOT MONOPLANE

Span: 29 feet 6 inches
Chord: 7 feet
Wing area: 183 square feet·
Weight: 760 pounds
Wing loading: 4¼ pounds per square foot
Power loading: 15 pounds per HP
Power: (A number of engines were used such as the 4 cylinder Clerget (50 HP) the 8 cylinder E.N.V. of 40 HP)
Speed: with the 50 HP Clerget 51 MPH

A passenger-carrying version of the Hanriot existed with a wing spread of 42 feet and a wing area of 300 square feet. Powered by a 6 cylinder aircooled Anzani that developed 45 to 60 HP, it weighed 1120 pounds and its speed was reported as being "somewhat less than the small type".

THE DEPERDUSSIN MONOPLANE 1911

Span: 28 feet 9 inches
Length: 23 feet 9 inches
Chord: 5 feet 9 inches
Power: Assortment of engines, Gnome, Anzani, Clerget.

DE PISCHOFF MONOPLANE

Span: 27 feet 6 inches
Length: 8 feet 3 inches
Area: 108 square feet
Weight: 720 pounds
Speed: 48 MPH
Power: 60-70 HP Austro Daimler

SANTOS-DUMONT'S *DEMOISELLE*
1909 model

Span: 18 feet
Length: 26 feet
Wing area: 115 square feet
Gross weight: 235 pounds
Wing loading: 2 pounds per square foot
Power loading: 3½ pounds per HP
Power: Darraq 2 cyl. 35 HP
Speed: 35 to 55 MPH

This little bug of a plane, nicknamed an "Infuriated Grasshopper", was the world's first light plane. Designed by Santos Dumont and flown by him on Sept. 13, 1909 from St. Cyr to Buc (France), 5 miles in 12 minutes at 180 feet altitude, the model later became popular as a crowd amuser at various air meets.

The pilot sat in a canvas sling, his posterior but inches from the ground, and operated his five controls, one of which required a special attachment on the back of his coat. Into this pocket ran the warping rod which controlled lateral motion. To bank, the pilot merely leaned in the direction of the turn. On his right was a vertical wheel. Pushing it forward turned the plane right; pulling it back turned it left. A second wheel to port controlled vertical direction. The throttle was operated by foot, and the spark regulated by a wire that hung down before him.

THE VALKYRIE RACER

Span: 31 feet
Length: 26 feet
Chord: 6 feet
Wing area: 190 feet
Wing loading: 3½ feet per square foot
Power loading: 22½ pounds per HP
Weight: 550 pounds
Power: Gnome 50 HP

BRISTOL *TEN SEATER*

Span: 54 feet
Length: 42 feet
Height: 11 feet
Weight empty: 3900 pounds
Weight loaded: 6800 pounds
Top speed: 122 MPH
Climb: to 5000 feet in 9 minutes
Ceiling: 13500 feet

HANDLEY PAGE *HP-42 HANNIBAL*

Span (upper wing): 130 feet
Length: 86 feet 6 inches
Total wing area: 2989 square feet
Gross weight: 29500 pounds
Payload: 8700 pounds
Wing loading: 9.86 pounds per square foot
Power loading: 15 pounds per HP
Power: Four Bristol *Jupiters* 2000 HP
Maximum speed: 120 MPH
Cruising speed: 105 MPH
Landing speed: 52 MPH
Climb: 600 feet per minute

THE DE HAVILAND *DRAGON RAPIDE*

Span: 48 feet
Length: 34 feet 6 inches
Height: 10 feet 3 inches
Area: 336 feet
Empty weight: 3230 pounds
Gross weight: 5500 pounds
Maximum speed: 157 MPH
Cruising speed: 132 MPH
Climb: 867 feet per minute
Ceiling: 16,700 feet
Ceiling (1 eng.): 3,100 feet
Range: 556 miles

DE HAVILAND *DH-50*

Span: 42 feet 6 inches
Length: 30 feet 9 inches
Height: 11 feet 7 inches
Area: 436 feet
Wing loading: 8.4 per square foot
Power Loading: 18.3 per HP
Maximum speed: 111.5 MPH
Landing speed: 57 MPH
Climb: 500 feet per minute
Power: 230 HP Siddley *Puma*

LOCKHEED *ELECTRA*

Span: 55 feet
Length: 38 feet 7 inches
Height: 10 feet
Area: 458 feet
Wing loading: 19.64 pounds per foot
Power loading: 10.71 pounds per foot
Gross weight: 10,500 pounds
Useful load: 5,046 pounds
Maximum speed: 221 MPH
Cruising speed: 203 MPH
Landing speed: 63 MPH
Climb: 1350 feet per minute
Ceiling: 20,000 feet
Range: 750 miles
Power: Two 420 HP Pratt & Whitney *Wasp Juniors*

CONSOLIDATED *FLEETSTER 17*

Span: 45 feet
Length: 31 feet 9 inches
Height: 9 feet
Wing area: 313 square feet
Gross weight: 5600 pounds
Pay load: 2157 pounds
Wing loading: 17.86 pounds per square foot
Power loading: 9.74 pounds per HP
Power: One P&W *Hornet* 575 HP
Speed: 180 MPH
Cruising speed: 153 MPH
Landing speed: 60 MPH
Climb: 1100 feet in one minute

FAIRCHILD *71*

Span: 50 feet
Length: 32 feet 11 inches
Height: 9 feet 4 inches
Wing area: 309 square feet
Gross weight: 5500 pounds
Useful load: 2370 pounds
Power: One P&W *Wasp* 420 HP
Power loading: 13.10 pounds per HP
Wing loading: 17.75 pounds per square foot
Speed: 129 MPH
Cruising speed: 103 MPH
Climb: 4990 feet in 10 minutes

FOCKE-WOLF *A-17a*

Span: 65 feet 6 inches
Length: 42 feet 6 inches
Height: 13 feet
Wing area: 672 square feet
Cabin length: 13 feet
Cabin width: 5 feet
Cabin height: 6 feet
Weight empty: 5380 pounds
Pay load: 3411 pounds
Wing loading: 13 pounds per square foot
Power loading: 18 pounds per HP
Top speed: 124 MPH
Cruising speed: 101 MPH
Landing speed: 66 MPH
Power: One Siemens *Jupiter* 480 HP

THE BREGUET *14-A2*

Span: 47 feet
Length: 29 feet 7 inches
Height: 10 feet 8 inches
Maximum speed: 118 MPH
Endurance: 4 hours
Passengers: 4
Climb: 16400 feet in 22 minutes
Weight empty: 2222 pounds
Weight loaded: 3380 pounds

BE2E

Span: (Upper) 40 feet 9 inches
       (Lower) 30 feet 6 inches
Length: 27 feet 3 inches
Chord: 5 feet 6 inches
Wing area: 360 square feet
Power: R.A.F. 90 HP
Speed: 90 MPH
Climb: to 1000 feet, 1 minute 36 seconds
Weight empty: 1431 pounds
Weight loaded: 2100 pounds

JUNKERS *F-13*

Span: 58 feet
Length: 31 feet 5 inches
Height: 11 feet 5 inches
Wing area: 430 feet
Total weight: 4,070 pounds
Useful load: 1,540 pounds
Power: Choice: from 160 HP to 230 HP. Most F-13s were powered by either a BFW of 185 HP or a Junkers 195 HP, both water-cooled.
Maximum speed: 125 MPH
Cruising speed: 106 MPH

AEROMARINE MODEL *50 C* FLYING BOAT

Span: 48 feet
Length: 28 feet
Weight empty: 2286 pounds
Weight loaded: 3276 pounds
Top speed: 75 MPH
Low speed: 45 MPH
Climb: 2200 feet in 10 minutes
Fuel capacity: 35 gallons
Power: One B-8 150 HP

The pilot of this model, claimed as the first cabin flying boat built for commercial use, sat in an open cockpit forward while his passengers occupied the cockpit behind. The latter was enclosed by a transparent cover, divided and hinged in the middle to permit access from either side.

AEROMARINE'S CONVERTED *F-5-L*

Span: (upper wing) 103 feet 9 inches
Span: (lower wing) 74 feet 4 inches
Height: 18 feet 9 inches
Wing area: 1394 feet
Takeoff: in 15 mile wind, 30 to 40 seconds

The F-5-L was a big, rugged dependable twin-engined tractor biplane. As a military plane its cruising radius had been 10½ hours, and fully loaded it weighed seven tons. Cruising radius was considerably reduced by Aeromarine by the removal of tanks and the substitution of passenger accommodations, but it was still capable of four and five hour flights.

It was powered by a pair of 400 HP *Liberty* engines mounted between the wings one each side of the fuselage, and the pilot's cockpit (located near the bow in the military version) was moved back under the wing between them.

THE *HS-2* FLYING BOAT

Span: 74 feet
Length: 40 feet
Height: 14 feet 7 inches
Wing area: 800 feet
Weight loaded: 6223 pounds
Useful load: 1864 pounds
Maximum speed: 91 MPH
Landing speed: 55 MPH
Climb: to 1800 feet in 10 minutes
Range: 575 miles
Wing loading: 7.7 pounds per square foot
Power loading: 18.8 pounds per HP
Power: One 330 HP *Liberty* pusher.

The HS-2 flying boat was built by Curtiss for patrol purposes. It was not a particularly outstanding war machine, and its use was limited to pilot training for the *H-16* and *F-5-L* boats, and for patrol work in the U. S. But it was a good performer and was easily converted to Aeromarine's work by cutting in two passenger cockpits immediately in front of the pilot and observers seats.

THE STOUT *2-AT*

Span: 58 feet 4 inches
Length: 45 feet 8 inches
Height: 11 feet 10 inches
Area: 600 feet
Wing loading: 9.85 pounds per foot
Power loading: 14.8 pounds per HP
Empty weight: 3638 pounds
Useful load: 2379 pounds
Duration: 4 hours
Ceiling: 10,000 feet
Climb: 5000 feet in 12 minutes
Top speed: 116 MPH
Cruising speed: 100 MPH
Power: One 400 HP *Liberty*

The *2-AT,* brain child of William Stout, designer of the Ford *Tri-Motor,* was America's first all metal passenger plane. When built in 1924 only 3 engines with any degree of dependability existed in the United States: the 90 HP *OX-5;* the 150 HP Hispano-Suiza and the 400 HP *Liberty*—all built in 1917 and 1918, and all war surplus. The *OX* and the *Hisso* were too small for this big monoplane; the *Liberty* too bulky and heavy. But the latter was chosen as the lesser of two evils, and as it turned out, gave the machine its fine safety record and above-average performance.

Eight passengers were accommodated in the spacious cabin in plain, but adequate seats. No effort was made to soundproof the interior or provide heat. Pilot and co-pilot sat forward in an enclosed cockpit on some models and an open one on others.

RYAN-STANDARD CABIN BIPLANE

Span: 40 feet
Length: 27 feet
Payload: 1000 pounds
Speed: 90 MPH
Landing speed: 40 MPH
Climb: 1000 feet in 1½ minutes
Ceiling: 10000 feet

This was a converted World War 1 *J1* Standard repowered with the 150 HP Hispano Suiza engine.

"Aviation" for 1924 described it as "clean cut in design and offers a very well proportioned and streamline appearance".

Cabin was finished in mahogany veneer and upholstered in Spanish leather. Flower vases and dome lights were standard equipment. The cabin top hingled upward to provide access, and its interior was unmarred by struts or pipes or rods.

Gas tank was placed on the top wing, and the pilot seat was raised enough to allow forward vision over the cabin.

THE RYAN-*CLOUDSTER*

Span: 55 feet 11 inches
Length: 36 feet 9 inches
Height: 12 feet
Weight: 9600 pounds
Speed: 120 MPH top
Range: 550 miles
Power: 400 HP *Liberty*
Wing area: 800 square feet
High speed: 110 MPH
Landing: 50 MPH
Wing loading: 8½ pounds per square foot
Power loading: 14½ pounds per HP

In 1925 Ryan converted this 1920 model into a 12-passenger plane by installing a row of five seats on each side of the cabin and a jump seat between the last two. The 12th passenger (if and when circumstances dictated) sat forward with the pilot. Baggage was carried in a compartment aft of the cabin.

HAMILTON

Span: 54 feet 5 inches
Length: 34 feet
Height: 9 feet
Wing area: 390 square feet
Weight empty: 3100 pounds
Load: 2300 pounds
Top speed: 135 MPH
Cruising speed: 115 MPH
Landing speed: 55 MPH
Climb per minute: 1250 feet
Ceiling: 18000 feet
Power: One P&W Wasp 400 HP
Passenger capacity: 8

THE STINSON DETROITER BIPLANE

Span: 35 feet 10 inches
Length: 28 feet 10 inches
Height: 10 feet 3 inches
Wing area: 354 square feet
Weight loaded: 3280 pounds
Weight empty: 1815 pounds
Top speed: 128 MPH
Cruising speed: 105 MPH
Landing speed: 55 MPH
Climb: 750 feet first minute
Ceiling: 13,500 feet
Fuel capacity: 90 gallons
Power: One 200 HP J-5 Wright Whirlwind
Seating capacity: 4 passengers and pilot.

The model SB-1 biplane was the first of a long line of four and five-place passenger-carrying planes designed and built by the late Eddie Stinson in Detroit. It was used extensively by a number of airlines on scheduled and non-scheduled work from Alaska to Mexico. First built in 1925, construction of these ships continued on into early 1927 when production was shifted to the SMB-1 Detroiter monoplane.

FOKKER F-10

Span: 71 feet 2 inches
Length: 50 feet 8 inches
Height: 12 feet 5 inches
Wing area: 728 square feet
Gross weight: 12500 pounds
Payload: 2640 pounds
Power: Three P&W Wasps, 1200 HP
Wing loading: 14.70 pounds per square foot
Power loading: 10.41 pounds per HP
Speed: 148 MPH
Cruising speed: 125 MPH
Landing speed: 55 MPH

BOEING 40-B

Span: 44 feet
Length: 33 feet 6 inches
Height: 11 feet 8 inches
Wing area: 545 square feet
Gross weight: 6080 pounds
Useful load: 2271 pounds
Wing loading: 11 pounds per square foot
Power loading: 11½ pounds per HP
Power: One P&W Hornet, 525 IIP
Speed: 135 MPH
Cruising speed: 110 MPH
Landing speed: 57 MPH
Climb: 800 feet one minute

BOEING 80-A

Span: 80 feet
Length: 55 feet
Height: 15 feet 2 inches
Wing area: 1250 square feet
Gross weight: 17500 pounds
Useful load: 7083 pounds
Wing loading: 14 pounds per square foot
Power loading: 11.6 pounds per HP
Power: Three P&W Hornets, 1575 HP
Speed: 138 MPH
Cruising speed: 115 MPH
Landing speed: 55 MPH
Climb: 850 feet per minute

THE FOKKER F-32

Span: 99 feet
Length: 70 feet 2 inches
Height: 16 feet 6 inches
Area: 1330 feet
Horse power: 2300 HP
Power loading: 10.6 pounds per HP
Wing loading: 18.23 pounds per foot
Weight empty: 15,080 pounds
Useful load: 9,170 pounds
Gross weight: 24,250 pounds
Top speed: 146 MPH
Cruising: 123 MPH
Landing speed: 60 MPH
Climb: 850 feet per minute
Service ceiling: 13,000 feet
Radius: 550 to 770 miles

The front engines turned 10 foot diameter, 2-blade adjustable steel propellers, while the rear engines, forced to work in the wake of their mates were equipped with 3-bladed props, 9 feet in diameter. Opposite rotation of the engines eliminated all torque.

THE TRAVEL AIR 6000

Span: 48 feet 7 inches
Length: 30 feet 10 inches
Area: 282 feet
Weight empty: 2375 pounds
Pay load: 944 pounds
Gross weight: 4000 pounds
Wing loading: 14.2 pounds per square foot
Power loading: 18.2 pounds per HP
High speed: 128 MPH
Landing speed: 50 MPH
Takeoff, full load, no wind: 720 feet
Landing run: 300 feet
Climb: to 5000 feet 12 minutes
Ceiling: 15000 feet
Range: 600 miles
Power: one 200 HP Wright Whirlwind

SIKORSKY S-38

Span: 71 feet 8 inches
Length: 39 feet 8 inches
Area: 720 feet
Empty weight: 5800 pounds
Gross weight: 8800 pounds
Top speed: 129.5 MPH
Cruising speed: 110 MPH
Landing speed: 52 MPH
Climb: 1000 feet per minute
Ceiling: 20,000 feet
Take off: (land) 7.5 seconds
Take off: (water) 14 seconds
Power: two 420 HP Pratt & Whitney Wasps

SIKORSKY S-40

Span: 114 feet
Length: 76 feet 8 inches
Area: 1740 square feet
Height: 23 feet 10 inches
Power loading: 14.8 pounds per HP
Wing loading: 19.5 pounds per foot
Empty weight: 21,300 pounds
Gross weight: 34,000 pounds
Payload: 8695 pounds
Maximum speed: 137 MPH
Cruising speed: 117 MPH
Landing speed: 65 MPH
Service ceiling: 11,700 feet
Climb: 800 feet per minute
Maximum cruising: 900 miles
Power: Two 575 HP Pratt & Whitney *Hornets*

1933 Model

Span: 82 feet
Length: 48 feet 10 inches
Height: 16 feet 1 inch
Area: 1208 sq. feet
Weight empty: 11465 pounds
Useful load: 6035 pounds
Gross weight: 17500 pounds
Top speed: 171 MPH
Landing speed: 62 *MPH*
Cruising speed: 145 MPH
Climb first minute: 850 feet
Cruising range: 560 miles
Absolute ceiling: 17500 feet
Power: 2 Wright *Cyclones,* R-1320F 700 HP each

LOCKHEED *AIR EXPRESS*

Span: 41 feet
Length: 27 feet 5 inches
Height: 8 feet 6 inches
Wing area: 275 sq. feet
Gross weight: 3645 pounds
Payload: 1000 pounds
Power: P&W *Wasp:* 400 HP
Wing loading: 13.25 pounds per sq. foot
Power loading: 9.11 pounds per HP
Speed: 167 MPH
Cruising speed: 135 MPH
Landing speed: 55 MPH

CONSOLIDATED *COMMODORE*

Span: 100 feet
Length: 61 feet 6 inches
Height: 14 feet 2 inches
Area: 1110 feet
Useful load: 7815 pounds
Fuel & oil: 2025 pounds
Pay load: 5270 pounds
Power, 2 Hornets: 1150 HP
Power loading: 15.3 pounds per HP
Wing loading: 15.85 pounds per foot
Top speed: 128 MPH
Cruising speed: 108 MPH
Landing speed: 55 MPH
Climb: 600 feet per minute
Climb 10,000 feet: 25 minutes
Service ceiling: 10,000 feet
Fuel capacity: 650 gallons
Radius: 1000 miles (light load)

FORD *TRI-MOTOR* MODEL *5-AT-A*

Span: 77 feet 10 inches
Length: 49 feet 10 inches
Height: 13 feet 8 inches
Empty weight: 6700 pounds
Disposable weight: 4100 pounds
Maximum speed: 130 MPH
Cruising speed: 110 MPH
Landing speed: 59 MPH
Power: Three P&W *Wasps:* 420 HP apiece
Passenger capacity: 11

BOEING *MONOMAIL*

Span: 59 feet 1 inch
Length: 41 feet 2 inches
Height: 16 feet
Gross weight: 8000 pounds
Payload: 3010 pounds
Speed: 158 MPH
Cruising speed: 140 MPH
Landing speed: 57 MPH
Climb: 720 feet per minute
Power: one P&W *Hornet* 575 HP

CURTISS *CONDOR*
1929 Model

Span: 91 feet 8 inches
Length: 57 feet 6 inches
Height: 16 feet 3 inches
Area: 1510 sq. feet
Weight empty: 11352 pounds
Useful load: 6026 pounds
Gross weight: 17900 pounds
Top speed: 138 MPH
Landing speed: 47 MPH
Cruising speed: 118 MPH
Climb first minute: 925 feet
Cruising range: 515 miles
Absolute ceiling: 19000 feet
Power: 2 *Conquerors,* 600 HP each

BOEING *247*

Span: 74 feet
Length: 51 feet 4 inches
Wing area: 836 square feet
Power: Two P&W *Wasps* 1100 HP
Speed: 180 MPH
Cruising speed: 165 MPH
Landing speed: 58 MPH
Climb: 8000 feet in 10 minutes

BELLANCA *AIRCRUISER*

Span: 65 feet
Length: 43 feet 4 inches
Height: 12 feet
Wing area: 654 square feet
Weight empty (landplane): 5983 pounds
Weight loaded: 10853 pounds
Max. speed (landplane): 165 MPH
Cruising speed (landplane): 155 MPH
Power: One Wright *Cyclone* 715 MPH
Passenger capacity: 11 to 14

    This big sesquiplane was the largest single engined plane of the day. Its cabin seated 11 to 14 and contained toilet facilities in the rear. There were three baggage compartments, one just forward of the pilot's compartment, and one in each wing stub.

THE BOEING *B-377 STRATOCRUISER*

Span: 141 feet 3 inches
Length: 110 feet 3 inches
Height: 38 feet
Area: 1769 square feet
Empty weight: 87,000 pounds
Gross weight: 145,800 pounds
Maximum speed: 375 MPH at 25,000 feet
Cruising speed: 320 MPH at 25,000 feet
Range: 2640 miles
Power: 14,000
Fuel capacity: 7,790 gallons
Consumption: 520 gallons per hour
Landing speed: 122 MPH

SIKORSKY *S-42*

Span: 114 feet
Length: 67 feet 8 inches
Height: 17 feet 4 inches
Wing area: 1330 square feet
Wing loading: 28.58 pounds per foot
Power loading: 13.57 pounds per HP
Empty weight: 21,945 pounds
Gross weight: 38,000 pounds
Payload: 8606 pounds
Maximum speed: 180 MPH
Cruising speed: 160 MPH
Landing speed: 65 MPH
Service ceiling: 16,000 pounds
Climb: 1000 feet per minute
Cruising range: 1200 miles
Power: Four 700 HP Pratt & Whitney *Hornets*

LOCKHEED *ELECTRA* TURBO-PROP

Span: 99 feet
Length: 104 feet 6 inches
Height: 32 feet 9 inches
Area: 1300 feet
Empty weight: 55,993 pounds
Gross weight: 116,000 pounds
Maximum speed: 450 MPH
Cruising speed: 406 MPH
Range: 3,000 miles
Power: 15,000 HP
Fuel capacity: 6,420 gallons (kerosene)
Landing speed: 130 MPH

MARTIN *M-130*

Span: 130 feet
Length: 90 feet 10 inches
Height: 24 feet 7 inches
Area: 2315 feet
Wing loading: 23.97 pounds per foot
Power loading: 16.23 pounds per HP
Empty weight: 25,363 pounds
Gross weight: 52,000 pounds
Useful load: 28,000 pounds
Payload: Varies with range
Maximum speed: 180 MPH
Cruising speed: 155 MPH
Landing speed: 70 MPH
Cruising range: 3000 miles (with 12 passengers)
Power: Four 830 HP Pratt & Whitney geared *Wasps*

BOEING *707-120*

Span: 130 feet 10 inches
Length: 144 feet 6 inches
Height: 38 feet 5 inches
Empty weight: 113,082 lbs.
Gross weight: 190,000 lbs.
Cruising speed: 589 MPH
Top speed: 610 MPH
Range: 4000 miles

THE BOEING *314 CLIPPER*

Wing span: 152 feet
Length: 106 feet
Height: 27 feet 7 inches
Weight empty: 49,641 pounds
Gross weight: 84,000 pounds
Top speed: 199 MPH
Cruising speed: 184 MPH
Maximum range: 5,200 miles
Service ceiling: 19,600 feet
Wing loading: 29.3 pounds per foot
Power loading: 13.1 pounds per HP
Power: 6,800 HP (Four *Cyclones*)

DOUGLAS *DC-8*

Span: 139 feet 8 inches
Length: 150 feet 6 inches
Height: 42 feet 3 inches
Area: 2758 feet
Empty weight: 128,013 pounds
Gross weight: 310,000 pounds
Cruising speed: 585 MPH
Range: 5100 miles
Fuel capacity: 23307 gallons

PHOTOGRAPHIC CREDITS

Page 2, Institute of the Aeronautical
Sciences
P. 12, Library of Congress
P. 13, Library of Congress
P. 14, (both) *Aeronautics*
P. 15, (top) *Flight*
(bottom) Hulton Press
P. 16, *Flight*
P. 18, (top) *Flying*
P. 19, (both) Brown Brothers
P. 20, *Scientific American*
P. 21, Smithsonian Institution
P. 22, (bottom) Smithsonian Institution
P. 23, Library of Congress
P. 24, (both) Library of Congress
P. 26, Library of Congress
P. 27, (top) Glenn L. Martin Co.
(bottom) Lockheed Aircraft Corp.
P. 28, Glenn L. Martin Co.
P. 30, (top) *Flight*
(bottom) Smithsonian Institution
P. 31, (top) Imperial War Museum
(bottom) *Flight*
P. 32, (both) *Flight*
P. 33, Monde et Camera
P. 34, *Aeronautics*
P. 35, Monde et Camera
P. 36, (both) Monde et Camera
P. 37, Hulton Picture Library
P. 38, (both) Monde et Camera
P. 39, (top and bottom right) *Flight*
(bottom left) Monde et Camera
P. 40, (both) *Flight*
P. 41, Institute of the Aeronautical
Sciences
P. 42, (top) Institute of the Aeronautical
Sciences
(bottom) *Flying*
P. 43, (top) *Flight*
(bottom) Monde et Camera
P. 44, (top) Library of Congress
(bottom) Monde et Camera
P. 46, (bottom) *Flight*
P. 47, (bottom) *Flight*
P. 48, (bottom) *Flight*
P. 49, (both) *Flight*
P. 50, (top) Bristol Aeroplane Co. Ltd.
(bottom) *Flight*
P. 51, (top) Bristol Aeroplane Co. Ltd.
(bottom) *Flight*
P. 52-53, (top) Handley Page
(bottom left) London Daily Mirror
(bottom center) *Flight*
(bottom right) Handley Page
P. 54, (top) *Flight*
(bottom) Bristol Aeroplane Co. Ltd.
P. 55, (top) *Flight*
(bottom) Picture Post Library
P. 56, (top) Picture Post Library
(bottom) *Flight*
P. 57, (bottom) *Flight*
P. 58, (both) *Flight*
P. 59, (top left) *Flight*
(top right) G. A. Broomfield
(bottom) *Flight*
P. 60, (top) A. V. Roe & Co. Ltd.
(bottom) Picture Post Library
P. 61, (top and bottom) *Flight*
(center) Short Brothers
P. 62, (center) *Flying*
P. 63, (both) Igor Sikorsky
P. 64, (top) Igor Sikorsky
(bottom) Library of Congress
P. 65, Underwood and Underwood
P. 66, Frederic Lewis
P. 67, (top) Henry W. Walden
(bottom) Smithsonian Institution
P. 68, (top) Glenn L. Martin Co.
(right) Smithsonian Institution
P. 69, Sperry Gyroscope Co.
P. 71, (both) *Flying*
P. 72, Institute of the Aeronautical Sciences
P. 73, Institute of the Aeronautical Sciences
P. 74, (top) Smithsonian Institution
(bottom) *Flying*
P. 75, (both) Smithsonian Institution
P. 76, (top) Institute of the Aeronautical
Sciences
(bottom) Smithsonian Institution

P. 77, *Flying*
P. 78, (top) Picture Post Library
(bottom) Monde et Camera
P. 79, *Flight*
P. 80, (top) Institute of the Aeronautical
Sciences
(bottom left) Monde et Camera
(bottom right) Smithsonian Institution
P. 81, *Scientific Age*
P. 82, (top) Smithsonian Institution
(bottom left) Monde et Camera
(bottom right) *Flight*
P. 83, *Flight*
P. 84, Hulton Picture Library
P. 86, (top both) *Flight*
(bottom left) K.L.M.
(bottom right) *Flight*
P. 87, Bristol Aeroplane Co.
P. 88-89, top (left) *Flight*
(top center) Handley Page
(top right) SABENA
(bottom left) Handley Page
(bottom center) Hulton Picture Library
(bottom right) Handley Page
P. 90, (top left) Handley Page
(bottom) Library of Congress
(right) *Flight*
P. 91, Bristol Aeroplane Co.
P. 92-93, (center) B.O.A.C.
(right) *Flight*
P. 94-95, (upper left) B.O.A.C.
(center) *Flight*
(right) B.O.A.C.
P. 94, (lower left) *Flight*
(lower right) Handley Page
P. 95, (both) *Flight*
P. 96, (all) *Flying*
P. 97, *Flight*
P. 98, (top) *Flight*
(bottom left) QANTAS
(bottom right) *Flight*
P. 99, through
P. 103, (all) Caproni
P. 104, *Scientific American*
P. 105, Air France
P. 107, (top) Monde et Camera
(center) Monde et Camera
(bottom) Air France
P. 108, (top) Hulton Picture Library
(bottom left and right) Institute of the
Aeronautical Sciences
P. 109, Mexicana de Aviacion
P. 110-111 (all) Mexicana de Aviacion
P. 111, (both) QANTAS
P. 112, (top left) QANTAS
(right) K.L.M.
P. 113, (top center) QANTAS
(top center and right) K.L.M.
(bottom) Underwood and Underwood
P. 114-115, (all K.L.M. except right center)
Institute of the Aeronautical Sciences
P. 116, Lockheed Aircraft Corp.
P. 117, Library of Congress
P. 118-119, (center) Hulton Picture Library
(right) Luft Hansa
(top left) Luft Hansa
(center and right) Inst. of the Aeronauti-
cal Sciences
P. 119, (right center) Inst. of the Aeronau-
tical Sciences
P. 121, Inst. of the Aeronautical Sciences
P. 122, (bottom) Underwood and
Underwood
P. 123, (top) SABENA
(bottom) British European Airways
P. 125, United Air Lines
P. 127, Ryan Aeronautical Co.
P. 128-9, (top) Smithsonian Institution
(left and center) Smithsonian Institution
(top right) Ford Motor Company
P. 128, (lower) Smithsonian Institution
P. 129, (center) Lockheed Aircraft Corp.
(bottom) Ford Motor Company
P. 130, Brown Brothers
P. 131, Underwood and Underwood
P. 132-3, (all) Ryan Aeronautical Co.
(map) Aeronautical Chamber of
Commerce
P. 134, (both) Ryan Aeronautical Co.

P. 135, (2) Northwest Orient Airlines
P. 137, United Air Lines
P. 138-9, (top left) Beech Aircraft Corp.
(center) United Air Lines
(right) Boeing Airplane Company
P. 138, (center) Underwood and
Underwood
(bottom both) United Airlines
P. 139, (bottom) TWA
P. 140, TWA
P. 141, J. J. Sloan
P. 142, (top left) TWA
(top right) J. J. Sloan
(center) Pan American Airways
(bottom) Lockheed Aircraft Corp.
P. 143, United Airlines
P. 144-5, (top left) Braniff Airways
(center and right) Institute of the
Aeronautical Sciences
P. 144, (bottom left) American Airlines Inc.
(bottom right) Curtiss-Wright Corp.
P. 147, (bottom) *Aviation*
P. 148, Ford Motor Company
P. 149, (top) Ford Motor Company
(both center) Mexicana de Aviacion
(bottom left) United Airlines
(bottom right) Ford Motor Company
P. 150, (top) Underwood and Underwood
(center) United Airlines
(bottom) Pan American Airways
P. 151, Convair
P. 152, (all) Convair
P. 154, Pan American Airways
P. 155, Pan American Airways
P. 156-7, (top left) United Aircraft
(center) Glenn L. Martin Co.
(right) Pan American Airways
P. 156, (bottom) Braniff Airways
P. 158-9, (top left) Boeing Airplane Co.
(both center) Ford Motor Company
(top right) Acme Photo
P. 158, (center) Institute of the
Aeronautical Sciences
(bottom both) Institute of the
Aeronautical Sciences
P. 159, (bottom) TWA
P. 160, (top) Braniff Airways
(bottom) SABENA
P. 161, *Aviation*
P. 162, Underwood and Underwood
P. 163, Mexicana de Aviacion
P. 164, Eastern Airlines
P. 165, (top) United Airlines
(bottom) V. C. Browne
P. 166, Braniff Airways
P. 168, (top) Los Angeles Airways
(bottom) Icelandic
P. 169, (top) Northwest Orient Airlines
(center left) Capital Airlines
(center right) Northwest Orient Airlines
(bottom left) British European Airways
(bottom right) NAC
P. 170, (top) British European Airways
(bottom) Glenn L. Martin Co.
P. 171, (top) Official U.S. Navy Photo
(center and bottom) Saunders Roe Ltd.
P. 172-3, (top left) Capital Airlines
(center) Mexicana de Aviacion
(right) N. Y. Airways
P. 172, (bottom) Los Angeles Airways
P. 173, (bottom) B.O.A.C.
P. 175, Institute of the Aeronautical
Sciences
P. 176, (top) Underwood and Underwood
(bottom left) Smithsonian Institution
(bottom right) Institute of the
Aeronautical Sciences
P. 177, (top) Hamburg American Line
(center) Institute of the Aeronautical
Sciences
(bottom) Smithsonian Institution
P. 178, (top) Underwood and Underwood
(bottom left and right) Brown Brothers
P. 179, (top) Underwood and Underwood
(bottom) Pan American Airways
P. 180, SABENA
P. 181, Eastern Airlines
P. 182, (top) Pan American World Airways
(bottom) United Airlines